P9-CQP-068

DEDICATION

The Animal within Us is dedicated to my parents who gave me the genes that caused me to think these ideas and write this book.

TABLE OF CONTENTS

ACKNOWLEDGEMENTS

Since I draw great sustenance from even minor interactions with people who have a smile and encouragement as part of their being, an attempt to thank all those who contributed to this book will fall short of the mark. The following are owed my sincerest gratitude and I doubt if the book would have ever seen the light of day without their unwavering support: Charlie and Jane Birmingham, Ron Brown, Craig Carlson, Alex Cilento, Sher Fuller, Gil Glass, the Ed Glass family, Pieter Halter, Donn Ketcheson, Don McCombes, gang at Main Beach, Paul Oleson, Steve Robinson, Freddie Schubeck, David Thoreau, Nancy Walker, Kevin Weaver, Roger Weninger, and Michael Zilz.

My ideas about the brain, mind, and human behavior have been shaped by time spent with Henry Hillman and Garth J. Thomas and the writings of Thomas Kuhn and Karl Popper. To whom I am greatly indebted.

PREFACE

Welcome to a book that I hope will be the source of significant positive changes in your life. It will provide you with fresh new insights into the origins of the thoughts you think, things you say, and actions you take as you go through the course of your life. These insights come from an appreciation of the influence that patterns of behavior we have inherited from our animal ancestors have over our own behavior.

Many of the concepts in the book would normally be found only in graduate-level seminars, the type attended by those working on their Ph.Ds. However, do not be alarmed. The language used is not technical and the ideas are explained in the context of the events of our everyday lives in a reader friendly and at times humorous fashion.

From my own experiences in graduate school and the experiences of many friends with medical and law school, I am convinced that what goes on in such higher education is mostly the learning of technical jargon, a shorthand way of communicating. The concepts are really not all that complex. For example, anyone capable of understanding plumbing can learn the concepts of the cardiovascular system. Anyone skilled at carpentry could function as an orthopedic surgeon.

However, in medical school, a jargon is learned that allows for a shorthand form of communication. "Ablate the sinoatrialnode" would have meaning only from one cardiologist to another even though the concept behind the words is really quite simple. "A discectomy at L3" speaks volumes from one orthopedic surgeon to another, yet given an explanation in plain English, anyone could understand what is meant.

The same principles of easily understood concepts encased in a "secret" jargon apply to law school and other graduate schools as well.

So fear not, reader. In the following chapters a story will be told, an easily understood and entertaining story, about how we can understand ourselves by looking to the behaviors of our animal ancestors.

The book is structured so the first two lessons present convincing evidence that we do have an animal-like brain in our human skull and it is this brain that controls the thoughts, feelings, and actions that we call *our selves*. Subsequent lessons take a look at our human feelings, behavior, and our cultural institutions and show how we can understand them by appreciating their origins in behaviors we share with animals.

The book's organization is based upon a comment by the great English novelist Lawrence Durrell: "I prefer to let my readers either sink or skim." Those who wish to skim may be content with simply reading the concise statement of each lesson to be learned presented at the beginning of each lesson. For those who wish to sink, the substance behind the lesson is presented in the pages that follow the lesson.

Of course I would urge the reader to sink. A thorough appreciation of the influence upon our thoughts and deeds of patterns of behavior we have inherited from our animal ancestors will open new worlds of understanding about how we cope with the daily events of our own lives. Taming and making friends with *The Animal within Us* is critical to our finding a psychological harmony in our lives.

INTRODUCTION

As a child, I was always fascinated by things mechanical. I was the kid who built his own go-kart out of a pile of nails, two-by-fours, wagon wheels, and an old lawn mower motor. I seem to have been born with a built-in need to understand how things work, to find out how all the bits and pieces interact, to work out how everything fits together.

Along with this inquisitive and analytical mind came a fairly labile mood. I remember that even in my early teens I would wake up one day feeling on top of the world and the next morning at the bottom of a deep hole. Of course I tried to understand these changes in a mechanistic way. I wondered: to what events in my life could I relate these mood swings, what were the bits and pieces that caused these troublesome changes and controlled my mood? I soon came to realize that my mood would alter independently of the events going on around me. Nothing in my life had changed from one day to the next, yet my mood would be quite different. Where, then, was the cause and effect?

When I was a teenager, an event happened that set the course for my continued quest and thirty-five years later brought about my writing *The Animal within Us*. In the late 1950s a family member was reading a book whose title I remember well, *Drugs and the Mind*. Written by Robert DeRopp and published in 1957, it was one of the first books for the lay audience that described the findings from the emerging field of biological psychiatry. DeRopp described some fascinating research that clearly showed that our mind and its emotions are related to the chemistry of our brain. Changes in one could be correlated with changes in the other.

At the age of fifteen, I had found a sign post that pointed in the direction of the solution to my own personal dilemma. The chemistry of my brain controlled my perception, my emotional response, to the events around me. I had been looking at the events themselves as the source for my mood, but that was the wrong place. The changes in my own mood/emotions may not have been related to the events of the day but instead may have been related to and caused by changes in the chemistry of my own brain. If only I could make measurements of my brain's chemistry, surely I would find the mechanistic solution, the bits and pieces, to explain the variations in my own mind's emotions.

Add another fourteen years to the story and I was graduating with a dual Ph.D. in neurobiology, the study of the brain, and psychology, the study of the mind. I was now set to pursue a lifetime of investigating the biology of the mind.

For the next eleven years I was an active participant in the academic world of neuroscience, doing research on the neurobiology of behavior—a scientific search for the bits and pieces of our moods, thoughts, and emotions, our human soul.

Life's happenstance events then led me to the world of venture capital, managing an investment fund that provides capital to start-up biotechnology companies. However, the time as a venture capitalist has not been time lost in my quest to understand the nature of the human mind. Anthropologists visit cultures around the world and look for the similarities and differences between them as a way to draw inferences about the common threads that run through our humanity. My dual careers have allowed me to play anthropologist, doing a cross-cultural field study. My years in the business world have been a hands-on internship in psychology.

The time spent in each of these two cultures, academia and private enterprise, has proved invaluable in my own search for an understanding of the human brain and what it produces, the human mind. Eleven years of watching and participating as humans interacted with each other in a world dedicated to searching for truth and knowledge

followed by fourteen years watching and participating as they interacted while maximizing return on investment, led to only one conclusion. On a personal level, the motivations and goals of the individuals are really the same. The drama of academia and the drama of
venture capital play on two different stages with very different scripts,
but the actors and actresses were fueled by the same fire.

Some people have a set of skills that allows them to achieve, to
dominate as scientists, others as investment managers. In both cases,
there is the need to win, and in both cases the politics, back-stabbing,
hype, and hustle used to achieve victory are similar. They are both the
same human animal, but in order to win the competition they have
chosen different careers that match their own individual skills. The
years spent in my own two different careers convinced me of the com-
monality of human motives and patterns of behavior and therefore of
their genetic and biological origins.

STATE OF THE ART

In the four decades after *Drugs and the Mind* was published, innumerable research papers have been written, and billions of dollars have
been spent in research on the brain and the mind. Our understanding of neurobiology has become incredibly more detailed during this
time, as has our understanding of psychology. However, at a concep-
tual level, little progress has been made in reconciling how the human
mind, with its emotions, conscious self-awareness, reasoned and logical thoughts, and spirituality relate to and are explained by the biology of the brain. The problem is one of explaining not only the origins of our human mind in our biological brain but also why the same
brain, in which reside our uniquely human mind and emotional life,
resembles so closely the brain of an animal.

This dilemma, the presence of our human mind, spirit, and soul
in our animal-like and purely biological body, is perhaps the greatest
mystery of life that is still left untouched by any credible attempts at
resolution. Certainly reams of data have been gathered on the biology
of human and animal brains and on human and animal behavior as

well. The differences between the animal and the human brain do not seem to be significant enough to explain why we have conscious self-awareness, a mind, and a belief in God, while the animals do not. Even though we now understand the biology of the brain at the level of its innermost genetic detail, we still have no clue as to how it produces all the varied pieces that taken together we call our human mind.

The Animal within Us presents a new theory to explain how the biological brain produces the human mind. A theory of the type I would like to propose is known in science as a "transfer equation." A transfer equation bridges the gap between two related but different ways of describing the same phenomenon. For example, if we know the temperature in degrees Celsius (C) and want to transfer the temperature to degrees Fahrenheit (F) we apply the following equation: $F = 9/5C + 32$. A transfer equation bridges the gap between one manner of description (Fahrenheit) with another manner of description (Celsius).

The Animal within Us develops a transfer equation to bridge the gap between the biology of our human brain and the thoughts and reasons of our human mind. In the chapters that follow we will travel a path that will sequentially add one concept to another until we have developed a transfer equation that will allow the body-mind duality to become a singularity. There is not a body and a mind, but only a singular process.

SOCIOBIOLOGY'S MISSING LINK

A genetic-biological-evolutionary basis for behavior is not a new concept. For many decades the field of sociobiology has been drawing parallels between patterns of human and animal behavior. Yet what is so clearly evident in this "dehumanizing" field is the lack of an explanation for the intellectual and emotional aspects of our human mind. So what if both chickens and corporations have a pecking order. The animals act on instinct, with no reasons, no feelings. We humans think, reason, and feel before we act.

It is all well and good for sociobiologists to show intriguing similarities between a human putting up a fence and "No Trespassing" signs and an animal marking its territory with its scent. However, we human beings are something more than mere animals acting on instinct. We humans think about what we do and we reason out how we should behave and we experience the emotions that accompany these behaviors. Sociobiology has its own *missing link: human reason*. *The Animal within Us* presents a revolutionary concept, a first-time answer to how our biological and animal-like brain creates the thoughts, reasons, and feelings that make us uniquely human.

VALUE

The Animal within Us covers a great many topics. It provides a basic scientific understanding of the forces of evolution, genetics, and neuroscience. In addition, it shows the origins of a variety of our thoughts and behaviors both at the level of the individual, such as religion and depression, as well as for human groups, such as international relations, in patterns of behavior we have inherited from our animal ancestors. Through it all, the goal is to provide you with insights into your own behaviors. The book is a self-help guide from the perspective of neuropsychology. It provides valuable lessons we can learn about our own lives from an understanding of the relationship between patterns of behavior passed on to us from our animal kin and our own human behavior.

Many self-help books serve a useful purpose, allowing us to see ourselves more clearly, but usually for only those parts of our lives specifically discussed in the book. By including the material on evolution, genetics, and neuroscience, I hope to give you sufficient background so you can continue to write for yourself the pages of the book that covers future events in your life.

You will become your own neuropsychologist and carry with you into the future the knowledge base that you need to draw useful conclusions about why we think and act the way that we do. You can watch yourself interact with your spouse, friends, colleagues, society, and the greater world at large—and perhaps see your own acts and motivations in a clearer light than was previously possible. It is for the sake of our own personal happiness that we learn from our animal brethren these lessons about life and use them to tame and to befriend *The Animal within Us.*

LESSON I

Our Humanity

From our earliest days to our modern times, we humans have always wondered about our origins and our place in the cosmos. We ponder the meaning of our lives and try to understand our thoughts and feelings. If we believe in the scientific method, which placed a man on the moon, allows us instantaneous global communication, and eradicated many plagues, then the answers to these questions must be found in the same way, the logical analysis of science. A true scientific answer to the origins of our human mind would provide us with valuable insight into why we think the thoughts, feel the feelings, and take the actions in our lives that we do. A scientific answer to the origins of the human mind is about the activity of the molecules and nerve cells in our brain. Yet for most of us there is something more to being human than just logic, molecules, and nerve cells. Our humanity, our thoughts, our feelings, and our immortal soul, could they simply be the by-product of the nerve cells percolating away in our brain? The same cells that are present in an animal's brain?

Copernicus (1473-1543) and Galileo (1564-1642) began a revolution in humankind's understanding of its own origins and place among the cosmos. Prior to their time it was a widely accepted belief that humankind and the planet earth were the center of a universe that was actively under the control of the hand of God. God created the heaven and the earth and could and would do whatever he wished with his universe and his people.

Copernicus and Galileo rearranged the world and altered humankind's sense of its own place in the cosmos when they proposed that the earth and its human inhabitants were not the center of the universe, nor were they under the control of the hand of God. Instead, the solar system obeyed physical laws, with the sun at the center and with the earth as only one of many planets that orbited the central sun. According to Copernicus and Galileo the heavens were governed by an order and lawfulness that were of a higher force than the hand of God. The church and the state, which at that time were one and the same, took great exception to these new ideas and saw to it that Galileo was brought to trial, convicted, and punished for such blasphemous ideas.

In the centuries following Copernicus' and Galileo's revolutionary proposals, the details have been filled in to show that they were on the right track. The earth and its inhabitants were certainly not the center of the universe; in fact, the earth is only one of perhaps billions of other planets, many of which may contain their own life forms.

To make matters worse for humankind's sense of uniqueness and self-importance, as well as for theology, Charles Darwin (1809-1882) added insult to the injury when he proposed that humankind was not God's creation but instead just a by-product of another natural force—evolution.

The ideas of Copernicus and Galileo removed the earth from the center of the universe and showed that it was controlled by forces above and beyond the hand of God. Now Darwin had shown that the presence on earth of human beings was not God's will but was also a result of natural forces. A revolution in our understanding of the place of humankind in the greater scheme of things had begun, and its aftershocks are still being felt today.

This revolution, however, is not complete. The past centuries of progress in our understanding of the laws of nature have confirmed and expanded the ideas of Copernicus, Galileo, and Darwin. However, in spite of all the evidence that there are only the laws of nature, atoms, and molecules, at some level we all still feel that humankind is special. We have a soul. We think, reason, create, love, and hate; we have hopes and aspirations for the future, and most uniquely, we have a consciousness that makes us aware of our individual thoughts, creations, loves, and hates. There must be more to our humanity than just atoms and molecules. We must be more than some monkey's relative.

BIOLOGY AND HUMANKIND

However, we humans do have to accept certain facts of life about the relationship between the biology of the human brain and our intellectual and emotional experiences as well as the relationship between our human biology and an animal's biology. Chemicals that affect our brain such as alcohol, LSD, or Prozac or a surgical alteration of the brain such as a lobotomy can have significant and quite specific effects upon our mental experiences, both intellectual and emotional. It therefore seems unequivocal that the contents of our human mind and our brain's biology are intimately related.

We have a heart that pumps life-giving blood throughout our body. This human heart is composed of the exact same chemicals and cells as is an animal's heart and serves the exact same function for humans as it does for animals. We are made of the same biological stuff as are animals, an inescapable conclusion.

The brain is one of the body's organs, just as the heart is one of the body's organs. It should not be surprising, therefore, that like the heart, our human brain is also little different from an animal's brain.

The chemicals and cells in a human brain are identical to the chemicals and cells in an animal's brain. Not only are the chemicals and cells the same but the way they are organized into the systems that control most of the body's basic functions are the same as well. For example, the neural circuits that control our sight, hearing, movements, eating, and reproducing are virtually identical to those of our nearest animal ancestors. *Yet, of course, it is this same animal-like human brain in which reside those things that make us uniquely human—our thoughts, our reasons, our feelings, our conscious self-awareness, our soul. Therein lies the problem.*

If our brain is so similar to an animal's brain and composed of only biological structures, then where does our humanity, our uniquely human consciousness and self-awareness, come from? We know we are human and they are animals. We each have a soul that we hope will go to heaven when we die. The animals have no soul, much less a concept of heaven or hell. We think, reason, and create. The animals do not. More importantly, we are consciously self-aware that we think, reason, and create. The animals simply exist and act on instinct.

Perhaps there is another dimension separate from science and its chemicals, a spiritual dimension? Maybe a spiritual force is added to our animal biology and that is what makes us truly different from animals and provides us with our human soul and our consciousness. That we still have these feelings about the uniqueness of our humanity is why the revolution begun by Copernicus, Galileo, and Darwin is not yet complete.

WHO ME?

The important and controlling influence of the animal-like and biological human brain over our behavior is there for all of us to see. Most intriguingly, it also creates the thoughts and reasons we use to *rationalize* our actions. The paragraphs below briefly describe some examples of how similar our behaviors are to those seen in our animal ancestors. The lessons to follow fill in the details and expand upon these examples.

As we make the transition from childhood to becoming a teenager we pass through the period known as puberty. Under the guidance of our genes, hormonal changes force our bodies to develop their adult male or female sexual characteristics. These same hormones force changes not only in our bodies but in our behaviors as well. Most typical is the behavior known as "teenage rebellion." This pattern of human behavior is really no different from the behavior of a teenage lion or chimp who strikes out on his own, driven by the same hormones as is the teenage human.

Teenagers have always had a host of complex and intellectual reasons to support their rebellion. To them it seems the only *rational* thing to do. These deeply felt rebellious teenage beliefs are under the control of genes and hormones in just the same way as is the development of facial hair for men and breasts for women. The match between a thought pattern and the biologically predestined behavior pattern leads the teenager to label that thought pattern as the rational one. To someone not under the control of the same hormonal surge, such as the teenager's parents, the same thought pattern will of course seem irrational.

Another example of the control of our thoughts and reasons by the behavioral programs we have genetically inherited from our animal ancestors is what we have come to call career burn-out, the mid-life crisis. The mid-life crisis relates to the animal behavior of dominance, a compelling need to have a position of status in a hierarchy, to be "top dog." The mid-life crisis is simply a middle-aged adult's realization that their dreams of dominance when they began their careers some 15 years earlier will never be achieved. When we make a mid-life career change for whatever complex and *rational* reasons, we are simply looking for another arena in which to try once again to become the leader of the pack.

The influence of our animal-like brain in our lives can show up in some very surprising places—cheerleaders, for example. Where do you think the idea for cheerleaders comes from? It is not a human invention. In book after book written by scientists who study animal behavior, one can read about chimpanzees that engage in battles over territory. The leader, the dominant male of one clan, goes toe-to-toe with the dominant male of another clan to slug it out for rights to a territory. In every instance of these battles, the females do not take part. They stay on the sidelines, jumping up and down, hooting and screaming, pumping up their champion. They are cheerleading chimps.

Even in conflicts between primitive human tribes the men square off against each other and the women are on the sidelines, cheering them on. Women do not fight in wars, either to the death or to the goal line. Mother Nature has given them a different role, cheering on the sidelines. Women, who are responsible for reproducing the species, cannot be killed off—no fool, Mother Nature.

The fundamental concept in our story is that we are a biological system, nothing more and nothing less. That concept has implications that many readers may find objectionable. We have seen that men fight the wars on battlefields and play their games in stadiums while the women stay at home or stand on the sidelines and cheer them on. This is not a recent invention or a sexist ploy by men. These different male and female roles have been true from the beginning of animal life. Our human biology has brought men and women to this destiny. These are the sorts of lessons we have to learn from our animal ancestors, brought to us by Mother Nature.

Readers sensitive to these issues can be assured that they will be significantly challenged by the ideas presented in this book as to whether Mother Nature wants us to be "biologically correct" or "politically correct." *Perhaps being biologically correct is every bit as important as and is certainly more natural than, being politically correct.*

Are there also biologically correct social-political systems in which it is only natural that humans should live? The animal behavior pattern of possessing and marking a territory sees to it that we have a place we can call our own, whether it be a fenced-in piece of land or an apartment that we personalize by decorating it in our unique way. The force of Mother Nature will even drive us to defend our territory to the death. We feel just as strongly about the possessions that we keep in our territory. They are our private property—intruders beware. Through millions of years of evolution, the process of survival of the fittest has seen to it that this type of program is in our brain. We need a territory with food and water that is ours and only ours in order to guarantee survival.

Any system that denies private property and possessions may be *politically correct* to some, but it is definitely not *biologically correct.* Indeed such communal political philosophies have been a brief blip in the time scale of human history and today exist mainly where enforced by military rule. As we shall see, these behavioral programs that we have inherited from our animal ancestors are strong forces that control even the social-political philosophies under which we live and organize our human groupings into nations.

Our consciousness, our self-awareness, our thoughts, and our feelings, are the attributes that make us humans. *The Animal within Us* will describe how these uniquely human traits can be explained as a direct outcome of our animal-like and biological human brain. All that we are, the sum total of our humanity, comes from the chemicals percolating away in our brain even, as described briefly in the next paragraph and more completely in Lesson VI, our prayers and our gods.

The universal animal sign of submission to the dominant male is the body crouched low to the ground with the head dipped forward. We have all seen our pet dogs approach us, their supreme beings, in this manner. However, when we humans kneel down in submission to the ultimate leader of the human pack, we call it prayer. It is no accident that we have chosen the words "supreme being" for God, the leader of the human pack. Is "God's [the dominant male] in his heaven [leading the pack], all's right with the world"—a wolf's thought as well?

BIOBEHAVIORAL IMPERATIVES

These behavioral programs of Mother Nature that we have inherited from our animal ancestors can be divided into three major types. Virtually all of the behaviors in which animals and humans participate that involve interactions with other creatures (separate from solitary activities such as eating) fall into one or the other of these three classes. They are the *biobehavioral imperatives*. They are just as imperative to our brain as is keeping our heart beating, maintaining body temperature, and finding food and water. They are the behaviors that have been finely honed over millions of years by the evolutionary processes of natural and sexual selection and that have allowed the human species to survive and avoid extinction.

First is the imperative to claim a territory and the objects within that territory as one's own. The boundaries of a territory are marked, and intruders are warned to stay out or face the consequences.

Second is the imperative to organize social groupings into a dominance hierarchy. At the top of the hierarchy is the *leader of the pack*. The other members of the group organize themselves into various positions of status under the dominant leader.

Third is the imperative that encompasses those behaviors relating to sexuality. A mate is chosen, mating occurs, and the young are reared. The male and female are genetically programmed to play different and very specific roles in each of these behaviors.

The biobehavioral imperatives determine our thoughts and our actions. Rebellious teenagers, mid-life crises, private enterprise, and our prayers to and belief in a supreme being are all examples of the biobehavioral imperatives creating our *reasoned* thoughts that then lead to our actions.

Knowledge and understanding purely for the sake of knowledge and understanding have their value. *The Animal within Us* provides this type of information about the brain and the mind. However, knowledge and understanding that have a practical application for improving our everyday lives is, of course, the highest goal of scientific inquiry. Just as Sigmund Freud ventured into the unknown world of the mind with the goal of providing people with insight into why they think and act the way that they do, we also have a similar goal.

An understanding of how the biobehavioral imperatives of territory, dominance, and sexuality create our human thoughts, feelings,
and behaviors will provide us with important insights into not only
our own personal motivations, thoughts, and actions, but also those
of the people with whom we share our lives. From this understanding
of the patterns of behavior we have inherited from our animal ancestors, comes lessons about life that should allow us to change our
behaviors so that we can lead a life in which we come closer to achieving our personal goals and aspirations.

LESSON II

The Animal Within Us

The brain cells and the way they are connected together in our human brain in order to produce our human reason, thought, emotions and conscious self-awareness closely resemble the cells and connections in an animal's brain. In the case of our nearest animal ancestors, primates, the two kinds of brains are amazingly similar. In the neural circuitry of the brains of our animal ancestors are the programs for the patterns of behavior that allowed them to win the battles of the survival of the fittest. These patterns have been finely honed for this purpose by tens of millions of years of evolution. Achieving the goals of these behavioral programs is just as imperative to the brain as is keeping the heart beating— both are imperative for survival. Our human brain contains these same imperative patterns of behavior, and it is just as compelled to achieve these goals as is an animal's brain. These programs are the biobehavioral imperatives of sexuality, dominance hierarchies, and territorial marking and they are at the basis of all our human thoughts, feelings, and actions.

Legend has it that once upon a time there was a poisonous spider sitting on the edge of a pond, and the spider wanted to cross to the other side of the pond. A frog came hopping by, so the spider asked the frog for a ride on its back across the pond. The frog said "okay" but only if the spider promised not to bite. The spider assured the frog that it would not bite because if it did and the frog died, the spider would drown as well.

Lo and behold, halfway out across the pond, the spider bit the frog, which then started to die. On the way under, the frog looked up at the spider and asked, "Why, why did you bite? You promised not to. Now we will both die." The spider looked down at the frog, shrugged all its shoulders, and said: "It's my nature."

The spider had inherited in its genes a program that led its brain cells to connect themselves into a specific pattern. As a result, when the spider sensed a certain type of stimulus, its brain caused it to act in a predetermined manner and bite the frog. The spider had no choice; it was a victim of its own nervous system. It had to follow its biobehavioral imperative and bite.

That biology is destiny applies not only to the simple behaviors of a spider's bite. A little rodent called a vole and the biggest of bears, the grizzly, are examples of how complex behavior patterns are also preordained by the information encoded in an animal's genes.

The vole's body contains many of the same hormones as does a human's. Altering the levels of these hormones in voles changes not only the biological aspects of their reproduction but also a variety of complex behaviors related to their sexuality. The bonding of the parents to the offspring, grooming behaviors, the promiscuity of the parents (voles are normally monogamous), as well as behaviors that may be described as "parenting" can be manipulated in a reliable fashion by altering their hormones.

These experiments with the vole show that the vole's patterns of sexual *behavior* are just as much under the control of its genes and hormones as are producing eggs and breast milk. Are the varieties of human parent-child and husband-wife behaviors also a function of varying levels of hormones?

The grizzly bear, although closely related to the black bear, is a separate species of bear. In general, both a grizzly and a black bear look and act the same, as do most other bears. However, each has unique characteristics, both biological and behavioral, that make each a separate species of bear. A grizzly has a hump on the back of its neck, a black bear has no such hump; a grizzly's coat is lighter in color than a black bear's coat; and a grizzly bear shows far more aggressiveness than does a black bear.

The grizzly's hump and the color of its coat are two physical differences that are passed on genetically from generation to generation and maintain the uniqueness of the species. Aggression, a behavioral characteristic that separates a grizzly from other bear species, follows the same pattern of genetic inheritance. A grizzly cub does not have to be taught to act aggressively any more than it has to be taught to grow a hump or a coat of a grizzled color. This behavior is passed on through the principles of genetics from one generation to the next, just as biological as is the growing of a hump and the color of its fur. Perhaps the same principles of genetic transmission apply to the behavior of aggressive humans.

SURVIVAL

It is important to understand that patterns of behavior did not develop by accident. They are the product of millions of years of evolution. The forces of evolution are focused upon achieving one primary goal: to evolve a species possessing the traits that will allow it to survive and reproduce itself and thus avoid extinction. To achieve these goals, the members of the species must be able to live long enough to produce offspring who, in turn, will survive long enough to continue the reproductive process. In addition to reproduction, if the traits did not provide for the animal to be able to survive within the constraints of its present environment and to adapt to changes that may occur in its environment, then the species would become extinct. As a species we owe our very survival to the imperative nature of these behavioral programs.

For example, it is biologically imperative to human survival that our brain maintains our body temperature of 98.6 degrees whether we are in a tropical rain forest or on a snow capped mountain. A man's testes must produce sperm and a woman's ovaries must produce eggs. Traits such as these that provide the biological systems for survival, reproduction, and adaptation are forever embedded in a species' genes, passed on from one generation to the next.

These same principles of survival and genetic inheritance are not only applicable to those systems we have always considered *biological* but also to those systems that control our *behavior* as well. Just as the neural circuits that control breathing, and the hormones that make gonads produce sperm and eggs have been fine tuned over millions of years of evolution to achieve the goal of survival, the same is also true for the *behavior patterns* that have allowed a species to win the battle of the survival of the fittest.

It is critical to appreciate that these behaviors are not learned by each generation from its parents. They are a part of an animal's genetic heritage. The genes contain the instructions that cause the nerve cells to connect themselves in circuits that force an animal to perform these behaviors. The three main categories of genetically inherited behavior patterns that allow a species to win the battle for survival are the *biobehavioral imperatives* of *sexuality*, *dominance hierarchies*, and *territoriality*.

OUR ANCESTRAL DEBT

We do have an animal within us. Our human animal is the end-product of tens of millions of years of evolution—an evolution whose goal is to select those traits that allow a species to survive and avoid extinction. It is easy to understand and to accept that our heart, kidneys, bones, and other *biological* organs evolved this way; it may be harder to believe that the same is true for the brain and the mind.

Indeed, one of the greatest students of behavior and the founder of the study of behavior known as ethology, Konrad Lorenz, said in his preface to a 1965 edition of Darwin's *The Expression of Emotions in Man and Animals*:

> This fact, which is still ignored by many psychologists, is quite simply that behavior patterns are just as conservatively and reliably characters of species as are the forms of bones, teeth, or any other bodily structure.
>
> That behavior patterns have an evolution exactly like that of organs is a fact...

I hope readers are intrigued by this brief glimpse into the reasons why we think and act the way that we do and can begin to see the value for their own lives in an appreciation of the biological origins of our thoughts and actions. With a further understanding as described in the following lessons of just how controlling each of the biobehavioral imperatives are over the thoughts and actions of our everyday lives, we can learn to make friends with the animal within us and get the animal to behave as we wish it to behave: *to bring out the best in our own personal beast.*

LESSON III

Dominance

Every animal group—the lion's pride, the wolf's pack, or the chimp's troop—is a tightly structured organization headed up by a dominant figure, typically a male. He wins this spot as top dog through a series of battles with other pretenders to the throne. In the animal kingdom his main role is to produce the next generation. He alone is allowed to mate. In this way evolution has seen to it that only the most robust of the species passes on his genes to the next generation. The dominant figure also has the main responsibilities for the safety and keeping the social order of the group. Whether it is a business, government, or social organization, virtually all human events that involve more than one person are based upon the structure of a dominance hierarchy. At the head of the hierarchy is the leader of the pack. You will be amazed how ever present and controlling this dominance pattern of behavior is in our own human activities.

The evolutionary processes of both natural and sexual selection work to insure that only the most robust examples of a species pass their genes on to the next generation. In that way, over time a species becomes stronger and stronger and the probability of that species' survival increases. The way this is accomplished is to have the males compete with each other in physical combat for the right to mate. The male rams butting their horns is an often-seen image of such a battle for top dog (sheep, in this case). The more physically robust a male then the better equipped he would be to fight his way to a high ranking. This position of dominance (known as the alpha male) gives him the right to mate with the females and therefore pass his most robust genes on to the next generation.

The highest ranking males not only have exclusive rights to mate with the group's females, but also rights to feed first from the kill, no matter who made it. A prime example is the male lion who takes no part in the hunt and kill—that is the female's role—but who feeds first and most. Along with these privileges come responsibilities as well, such as marking and defending the group's territory from intruders. In this way, over time the genes of the fittest to survive become a greater and greater percentage of a species' gene pool, a necessary process if a species is to remain strong in order to survive and avoid extinction.

The females within a group also organize themselves into a hierarchy. The dominant female is the preferred mate for the dominant male. The lower-ranking females mate with the lower-ranking males if they are allowed by the dominant male and female to mate at all. Access to food is also a function of the female's position in the hierarchy. In a lion pride the higher-ranking females get to feed first from the fresh kill.

HUMAN HIERARCHIES

In one way or another at most times in our lives, we humans are also involved in activities whose goal is to maintain our status, our place in a dominance hierarchy. Personal happiness, our sense of self-fulfillment, pride, and self-esteem are intimately related to how successful we are in defending our status against the challenges from others below us and winning the challenges of our own making against those above us.

It should not be hard for readers to find an event within the last few days that reflects the role of such dominance and status issues in their own lives. There is no doubt that some feeling of self-esteem or some psychological hurt has occurred recently that had its origins in our putting someone in his/her place or finding a higher place for ourselves. We all hate to be "put down." The battlefields of these personal wars for status are littered with the psychologically wounded.

The imperative nature of our need to participate in a dominance hierarchy is at the core of one of the essential activities of commerce. Advertising controls the choices we make every day by appealing to our need for dominance and in particular, how the dominance imperative interacts with the imperative for sexuality. Companies rarely advertise products based upon the quantitative performance of their product versus the performance of a competitor's product. Instead, they make use of our need to achieve dominance as a way of attracting a mate. If you wear this type of shirt the advertisers claim, you will be the coolest dude around and the women will swoon. If you drive this type of car, drink this type of beer, smoke this type of cigarette, ...ad nauseam, you will be the coolest stud or the sexiest women and any man/woman of your choosing will be yours. Think about the car you drive, the clothes you wear, the athletic shoes on your feet, the street you live on—did status have anything to do with these choices?

Even our ancestors, the chimps, have been known to be susceptible to the same type of behavior. Although it came about purely accidentally, the following event described in Jane Goodall's *Through a*

Window, shows how a chimp used a product to enhance his display as the dominant male.

When Mike deposed Goliath and rose to the top-ranking position of the community Figan was eleven years old and clearly, fascinated by the imaginative strategy of the new alpha. For Mike, by incorporating empty four-gallon tin cans in his charging displays, hitting and kicking them ahead of him as he ran towards his rival, succeeded in intimidating them all—including individuals much larger than himself.

All the chimps were impressed by these unique, noisy and often terrifying performances. But Figan was the only one whom we saw, on two different occasions, "practicing" with cans that had been abandoned by Mike. Characteristically— for he was a past master at keeping out of trouble—he did this only when out of sight of the older males who would have been intolerant of such behavior in a mere adolescent...

An article in a magazine described the intricacies of dining in restaurants in Los Angeles and showed just how far we humans go in creating opportunities within our social order to flaunt our status. According to the article, which restaurant one eats in is only the first stage of claiming one's position in the hierarchy. Of equal importance is the table at which one is seated. Even which chair at the table is an indicator of one's position within that culture's hierarchy. Since I knew nothing of that culture, I must admit that when I began to read the article I assumed it was a spoof of such things, only to soon realize that it was a reality among certain social groups in Los Angeles.

Most of us probably have participated in situations or certainly heard stories similar to the one that I am about tell. I have a hobby of restoring old cars. There are car clubs for different makes of old cars— not only for different makes, but also for different models of each make as well as, in some cases, different clubs for those who race and those who just keep their cars shiny and go on Sunday drives. Needless to say, those who race feel more manly than and look down upon and feel dominant to those who use their cars as "garage decorations."

Once upon a time there was probably just a single club for each type of car. However, someone whose genes gave him/her a strong need for dominance that was not being satisfied through work or other activities came up with the rationalization as to why a separate club was needed for a particular purpose. Of course, that someone would be all too happy to serve as *President* of the club. Thus came the successive division of clubs into finer and finer sub-clubs, each with its own leader of the pack.

The Asian cultures use the concept of "saving face" as a fairly common thread throughout many of their social rituals. Those cultures where saving face is a common idea also have a history of a society organized along rigid hierarchical lines, where one's position in the hierarchy is a critical part of one's self-esteem. To "lose face" is the greatest personal emotional crisis one could ever face.

The following real-life episode illustrates the intense interaction of male and female dominance hierarchies in the Asian culture. A recent documentary program by the British Broadcasting Corporation about the deceased former Chinese ruler Mao Tse-tung showed just how human it is for the dominant male to have access to the all-too-willing females and for the females to compete to be chosen by the dominant male. The producer of the show, Jeremy Bennett, said, "In public Mao espoused the cause of human rights, in private he collected, used and discarded concubines in the hundreds." Mao's physician is quoted as saying, "Women felt honored to have sex with Mao, it was a great and natural thing to do because Mao was God and the supreme ruler. A relationship with such a man was very glorious."

LEADER OF THE PACK

In Lee Hall's fascinating biography, *Elaine and Bill,* of one of the great men of American art, Willem (Bill) deKooning, she describes the art scene in Greenwich Village, which at that time was the hub of the avant garde in American art. Many passages in the book call to mind a wildlife biologist's account of the hierarchical social order of a pack of wolves. In the following passages quoted from the book, the reader should note that Elaine is Willem's wife, an accomplished artist in her own right, and that the brackets are added for identification of the characters.

> Elaine became a gregarious woman who enjoyed power and dominance
>
> She was competitive in other ways as well... "I was so competitive" she boasted "that I learned to administer competition"
>
> Elaine liked a lot of artists, but only one could be king,...and from the beginning Elaine was going to make sure that Bill was king. Elaine, say friends who remember her early admiration for Bill, was equally determined to be the queen to Bill's king.
>
> the would be dukes and earls, the knights-errant, the court jesters, magicians, ladies-in-waiting were assembling. As they displayed their costumes and manner, their wares and talents, Elaine and Bill looked them over and formed friendships, alliances of convenience, and social pacts.
>
> They [Elaine and Bill] were very competitive—and they were determined to be the top dogs.

The main rival to Willem deKooning for his position as top dog, king, and dominant male of the art tribe was Jackson Pollock. In describing their interactions, Ms. Hall writes,

> When Jackson sold a painting, recalls an artist, "he couldn't wait to swagger into the Cedars [a local bar and hangout for artists] and flash a big roll of bills. The fool even liked to compare his initials—J.P.—to those of J.P. Morgan. What he was doing to the guys at the bar, of course was boasting about his masculinity. It was like this: "he was a tough hombre from out west—a go getter, a shit-kicker,—and he had taken on this

two bit fag town. He had money. Money meant power. And money and power implied sex, virility. That galled the hell out of deKooning."

In the early days of her affair with Pollock, Ruth [Pollock's girl] met Bill at the Cedars. "Bill razzed Jackson about Ruth," recalls an observer. "He pretended to grab at Ruth, and he rather lewdly suggested that Jackson had got hold of more woman than he could handle. Bill treated Ruth at that time like an insensate object—like some kind of trinket or toy that Jackson had—and he really went after Jackson's balls with a verbal knife."

They [deKooning and Pollock] would get drunk, be abusive and violent to one another at the Cedars, and just end up by each making a big show of taking some girl home for consolation.

each [deKooning and Pollock] stood at the front of an army of spearbearers, foot soldiers, storm troops, and trampy camp followers

....Territories were marked, bets taken, troops deployed, and battles staged and recorded.

I read Ms. Hall's fascinating book with stunned disbelief. I wondered if she had a behavioral sciences background. Here was a description of two males vying for dominance. Females were also vying for dominance by aligning themselves with the dominant males. A legion of others who ranked lower on the dominance scale allied themselves with each dominant male's tribe, exactly like a pack of wolves or chimpanzees. All this was occurring not on the Serengeti plain or the tundra of Alaska but within the most intellectual and high minded of pursuits, exploring the cutting edge of avant garde art in the heart of New York City's skyscrapers.

MID-LIFE CRISIS

The term "mid-life crisis" is one often heard to describe the career angst of thirty to forty year olds. Now that we understand the driving force of dominance hierarchies in controlling our behavior, the mid-life crisis can take on a whole new perspective.

As we age and enter early adulthood, we choose a career at which we intend to spend a substantial portion of our lives. In our minds we expect to start at an entry-level position but we expect over time to gradually attain higher and higher stations within our career/company. In the beginning we only have dreams of future dominance. By the time we have arrived at our mid-thirties, we begin to get a pretty good sense of what the future holds for us. For some, it appears that our original dreams of achievement will probably not come true—a very difficult and painful realization. We perceive that the dominance to which we aspire may never come our way. Does our mind experience this perception as the *mid-life crisis* and do we then think our way through to a mid-life career change in response to our sense that we will not become king of that particular hill?

The mid-life crisis with all its high-minded reasons and emotionality represents another example of how the drive of the biobehavioral imperatives shape our thoughts, our reasons, and our feelings, and thereby controls the actions that we take.

Territories

Each animal group lives in a well-defined territory. The group marks the territory and defends it against intruders. It is easy to see why such a pattern of behavior is imperative to a species' survival since within the territory are the natural resources so necessary for the group's survival, such as food and water. We humans are also notoriously territorial: "Good fences make good neighbors." Our territorial instincts are not limited to defining boundaries but include ownership and control of the possessions within that territory, our private property. The political system of capitalism owes its origins to this imperative we have inherited from our animal ancestors. Communism may be politically correct to some, but it is not biologically correct. Mother Nature in the form of the territorial imperative may have been responsible for its downfall.

The marking of a territory is the responsibility of the dominant male and it defines the areas in which the dominant male and his group can exert their rights. These rights are not just to the territory but include the food, water, and shelter, the *private property* within the territory. Along with these rights goes the responsibility of the dominant male to defend the territory and its property from intruders. The leader of the pack protects his extended family from rape, pillage, and plunder. This pattern of behavior is an imperative. If territories are not aggressively defended, the resources within the territory would be available to everyone and therefore they may not be sufficient to anyone for their survival.

In the book, *Never Cry Wolf,* that became a feature movie, Farley Mowat describes his own territorial tussle with a dominant male wolf.

In any event, once I had become aware of the strong feeling of property rights which existed amongst the wolves, I decided to use this knowledge to make them at least recognize my existence. One evening, after they had gone off for their regular nightly hunt, I staked out a property claim of my own, embracing perhaps three acres, with the tent at the middle, and *including a hundred-yard long section of the wolve's path* [emphasis added].

Staking the land turned out to be rather more difficult than I had anticipated. In order to ensure that my claim would not be overlooked, I felt obliged to make a property mark on stones, clumps of moss, and patches of vegetation at intervals of not more than fifteen feet around the circumference of my claim. This took most of the night and required frequent returns to the tent to consume copious quantities of tea; but before dawn brought the hunters home the task was done, and I retired, somewhat exhausted to observe results.

I had not long to wait. At 0814 hours, according to my wolf log, the leading male of the clan appeared over the ridge behind me, padding homeward with his usual air of preoccupation. As usual he did not deign to glance at the tent; but when he reached the point where my property line intersected the trail, he stopped as abruptly as if he had run into an invisible wall. He was only fifty yards from me and with my binoculars I could see his expression very clearly.

His attitude of fatigue vanished and was replaced by a look of bewilderment. Cautiously he extended his nose and sniffed at one of my marked bushes...

He appeared to take the hint. Getting to his feet he had another sniff at my marker, and then he seemed to make up his mind. Briskly, and with an air of decision, he turned his attention away from me and began a systematic tour of the area I had staked out as my own. As he came to each boundary marker he sniffed it once or twice, and then carefully placed *his* mark on the outside of each clump of grass or stone...

Once it had been formally established and its existence ratified by the wolves themselves, my little enclave in their territory remained inviolate. Never again did a wolf trespass my domain. Occasionally, one in passing would stop to freshen up some of the boundary marks on his side of the line, and not to be outdone in ceremony, I followed suit to the best of my ability...

For a species to survive, it was necessary to have a biobehavioral imperative that would force it to protect the territory and the property within it that satisfied both its nutrient needs as well as its reproductive needs. Even though our own human survival in the twentieth century may no longer be dependent on our marking and defending a personal territory, this behavior pattern is still a part of our genetic heritage. Its critical role in the survival of our species has not been forgotten by the neural circuits of the human brain; it is still imperative that we act territorially. Indeed, under the control of this imperative, we humans have created an elaborate system of laws and social institutions to allow us to act in a territorial fashion.

Any property owner is all too aware of the laws and procedures that we humans have established to allow us to act upon this imperative to mark and to defend a territory as our own. Once we have signed the paperwork, the territory is ours and we then communicate its boundaries to others. Whether it is a fence around our own property or a security gate leading into our community, we let others know, "No Trespassing." To use scent marks for boundaries, as did our animal ancestors, would of course be considered uncivilized. In our civilized society we cannot warn trespassers to leave our property by jumping up and down and screaming threats at them as animals do. We have developed other socially acceptable behaviors to accomplish the same goal.

The watchdog is a traditional surrogate for the animal within us. It is considered only natural for a dog to bark at an intruder. Indeed, we even mark our boundaries with signs that say "Beware of Dog." He will perform his own natural territorial defense, one that is encoded in our brain as well, but that social convention will not allow us to express.

There are many of us, however, who are not owners of a specific piece of land that we can mark and defend. We may be renters in an apartment complex of numerous other like apartments, with no obvious signs of demarcation other than the number on the door of our apartment, which is different from the number on the doors of all the other similar apartments. Driven by the territorial imperative, in spite of the seeming lack of a true territory to mark, we will go to great lengths to individualize an apartment and to do our best to create a sense of our own personalized territory. The notion of decorating our own apartment is often described and explained as "reflecting one's own life style." The more individualized and distinctive that we make our apartment, the more reflective of a strong need within us to express this imperative.

For example, teenagers with their raging hormones are compelled to differentiate their territories from those of their parents, it is only natural. Thus, parents should not thwart their teenagers from covering their bedroom walls with posters. Within the boundaries of propriety these territorial-marking behaviors should be encouraged as a way for teenagers to develop a sense of their own identity and a necessary stage for teenagers to successfully pass through on their way to becoming fully functioning adults.

MY COUNTRY RIGHT OR WRONG

For animals, battles over the rights to territories are resolved through nonlethal behavioral displays. Through the signs and symbols of dominance and submission know only to that species, one dominant male exerts his power over another dominant male and the rights to the territory are for him and his followers alone. The loser and his troop must leave. It is rare that such struggles end in death.

Humans, however, have raised territorial battles to the level of lethal combat more as the rule and not the exception. Over the course of human history, the tens of millions of dead on battlefields attest to the ongoing presence within our human brain of the animal need to mark and defend a territory. Just as the book by Ms. Hall described human interactions as if the people were a wolf pack engaged in dominance struggles, when reading *Histories*, written in the fifth century *B.C.* by the Greek historian Herodotus, I had the same feeling that I could just as easily be reading about wolves as about humans. The book describes how the early Greek city-states engaged in wars for territory. Change a few names and it would read as if a wildlife biologist were describing how different packs of wolves engage in their territorial behaviors.

The intensity of the imperative for territory within our human brain is reflected in the saying "my country right or wrong"—who cares about rationality, it is my territory and I must give my life to protect it.

PRIVATE PROPERTY

The drive to mark and defend our territory applies to the possessions we keep within the territory as well. The possessions within our territory are just as sacrosanct to us as is the territory. Although we are taught when we are young to share and not to be selfish, our imperatives give us a natural inclination to keep what is ours to ourselves. Sharing for most of us is terribly hard to do. It has even become commonplace to make jokes about the annoying intrusiveness of the neighbor who is always borrowing something. We have no reason not to share, but our biobehavioral imperative wants us to protect and to hoard what is within the boundaries of our own territory. For animals and primitive peoples with a scarcity of resources hoarding is a behavior necessary for survival, but for twentieth century humans living in a time of abundance it is testimony to the control by the biobehavioral imperatives over our thought processes.

We should not feel bad that we are not more charitable with our possessions. As the following example shows, just as with many other behaviors, our selfishness is also a part of our genetic inheritance. We are not the only primate that is selfish.

In order to investigate the learning capacity of chimps, scientists invented a device called a "Chimp-o-Mat." When the chimp pressed the correct button, he would receive a plastic poker chip that could later be traded in for food. The brighter chimps soon began to collect and hoard their excess chips. If a chimp tried to steal a chip from another chimp, all hell would break loose as the owner would fiercely protect his earnings from the thief.

Charles Darwin in *The Descent of Man* also describes the source of our selfishness in our nearest animal relatives:

> In the Zoological Gardens, a monkey which had weak teeth, used to break open nuts with a stone; and I was assured

by the keepers that after using the stone, he hid it in the straw, and would not let any other monkey touch it. Here, then, we have the animal origins of the human idea of private property; common to every dog with a bone, and to most or all birds with their nests.

COMMUNISM AND CAPITALISM

These imperatives we inherited from our animal ancestors play an important role in the way we organize our human societies. Their significance is well demonstrated by the recent collapse of the Soviet Union's communal political system. The Soviet Union imposed a communal political philosophy on its people, denying individuals private property and possessions. When these formerly communist countries were freed, the animals within their peoples grasped the notion of private property with open arms.

Needless to say, in the context of human history such political systems have had only the briefest of appearances. Today, only the rule of force keeps a few countries under a communal political system. Perhaps from this example we are once again reminded of the force of Mother Nature. A biobehavioral imperative is no different from a hurricane or an earthquake, a force of Mother Nature. To get in her way is not a wise thing to do.

LESSON V

Sexuality

For a species to survive and not become extinct, there is no greater imperative than its ability to produce the next generation. Mother Nature could not leave reproduction of the species to chance so she hard wired the patterns of behavior that accomplish reproduction into our genes, and she gave men and women quite different roles to achieve this goal. We all recognize that on average men are taller than women, a statistical fact, and a valid gender stereotype. It is also a fact that an individual woman may be taller than an individual man and is known as "biological variability." An appreciation for the way that statistical averages lead to gender stereotypes and biological variability leads to individual gender differences provides us with tremendous insight into the different behavioral predispositions Mother Nature has chosen for men and women. If Mother Nature had left these patterns of sexual behavior up to chance, our species would have been relegated to the boneyard of extinction. In the case of gender differences in patterns of behavior between men and women biology must surely be destiny since the fate of the human race is at stake.

There is no biobehavioral imperative that is more important and controlling of our behaviors and more responsible for the way we have designed our human cultures than is the one related to our sexuality. How much of your day is spent either thinking or acting on matters sexual? Our preoccupation with sex is easy to understand since without a biobehavioral imperative that leads first to the act of reproduction, second to the gestation of the fetus, and third to the maintenance of the young, a species could not exist. It would fail to perpetuate itself and face extinction.

The behaviors related to reproduction, as is fitting given their essential role in survival, show an incredible array of complexity that begins with the male and the female finding each other and culminates in the production and rearing of the newborn. These behaviors in animals follow a rigid pattern that, as was described previously for the vole, is under the strict control of specific hormones. The complexities and subtleties of these hard-wired behaviors are shown in dramatic detail by the mating rituals of an animal known as the Tasmanian devil, a marsupial as is the kangaroo.

At the start of the mating season, the male devil, who lives alone, goes out at night and finds a female whom he pursues and harasses until she accompanies him into his own territory. For the next two weeks he will keep her inside his den, not letting her venture out. No wonder it is the Tasmanian *devil*. This two-week period of male-enforced captivity provides the stimulus to induce ovulation in the female. Until this two-week period has passed, she is not physiologically ready nor behaviorally receptive for mating. At the end of this two-week period, the hormonal changes evoked by this captivity will have caused her sex organs to undergo the changes that allow for fertilization of the egg. She will then mate with the male, and the young will be born approximately two months later. The young live in the mother's pouch until they are fifteen weeks old, at which time the parents dig a hole in the den in which the young will then live.

For the next several months, the parents live like a married couple, with both parents taking on the responsibilities for feeding and guarding the young. When the youngsters are approximately nine months of age, all bonds within the family break down. The parents separate from each other and the pups from the parents. Each parent returns to a life of solitude for the next several months until the mating season and the inevitable ritual begins anew.

There are no books on how to attract a mate or on parenting for Tasmanian devils to read. The highly ritualized and complex reproductive process that occurs over nine months is contained within a program in their brains. This program, in accordance with the instructions in the genes, was laid down during early development and finalized by the hormonal events that occurred during the time of puberty. This is but one example of how the complex and precise sequence of behaviors relating to choosing a mate, breeding, and rearing the young is totally under the control of hormones interacting with the neuronal circuitry of the brain. The same is true for each and every species in the animal kingdom. Have you ever been paid the ultimate compliment by your sex partner: "You're an animal."?

CHECK ME OUT

We humans, both men and women, go through mate selection rituals that put our animal ancestors to shame. Just as with the animals, these behaviors begin once hormonal changes occur during puberty. As a result of these hormonal changes, our thoughts and our actions change dramatically. It is almost as if there had been a brain transplant. We begin to pay attention to the sorts of things that allow us to present our "mating display" to the opposite sex. Mating and its associated behaviors dominate our lives, our thoughts, and our dreams.

For women this change typically involves behaviors related to their physical appearance. Interestingly, throughout time and in all cultures red seems to be the preferred color women use to attract men, from the naturally occurring colors of the tribes that depended on primitive colorings found in their environment to the bright reds of the lipsticks and nail polishes that our sophisticated technologies create. Throughout all human cultures, throughout all of recorded human history, at the time of puberty girls begin to use a variety of color enhancements to present their display to men. Facial painting by women as a way to attract men was not thought up by an advertising executive on Madison Avenue. Biology is truly destiny.

Postpuberty women will also use their newly emerging secondary sex characteristics, such as breast development and the curvaceousness of their bodies, to appeal to the opposite sex. Women put a great deal of effort into choosing their clothing, not for the functions of warmth, convenience, and longevity, but for its attributes in presenting their curvaceousness to men. For most women, from the time of puberty until a permanent mate is selected, sex appeal to men will typically become one, if not the main, preoccupation of this time period in their lives.

Men are equally involved and preoccupied with developing themselves as attractive sex objects to women. Again, beginning at the time of puberty, when changing hormones and the appropriate brain circuits interact, the concerns of the male teenager shift dramatically. Men do not bang their horns together as do rams in a head-to-head combat. No indeed. Our human brain/mind has developed complex ritualized activities to serve the same purpose.

Among men, the displays of sex appeal to women are mostly one or another sign or symbol of physical prowess and power over others. Teenage boys begin to work out, to build their muscles. They engage in any one of a variety of sporting events to show their physical prowess. Whether it is baseball, football, soccer, tennis, or basketball, most male teenagers are engaged in competitive activities that relate to their physical prowess. In other ways as well they vie with one another to be seen by females as objects of their sexual desires as the leader of the pack.

A major theme of this book is the appreciation that we humans have developed social structures and institutions to allow us to play out these imperatives inherited from our animal ancestors in socially acceptable ways. A primitive physical combat amongst males or a display competition between females for dominance and rights to mate with the opposite sex is not acceptable in our human society. *Our biological brain creates new ways for us to sublimate these biobehavioral imperatives and to divert them into a socially acceptable format.* This process is never more true than in the variety of behaviors that we humans have created in order to allow us to show ourselves as desirable mates to the opposite sex.

BEAUTIFUL PEOPLE

The women tend to be blond, their faces painted with bright colors, and their clothes designed to show their curvaceousness to maximum advantage. Many will even go to the length of having surgical procedures performed under anesthesia in order to enhance their curvaceousness.

The men have all acquired great wealth and/or power, the most common attributes that males use to attract females. They drive the fastest and most expensive cars, wear the most expensive and stylish clothes, and present themselves to the females as leaders of the pack. These men and women find each other. They all contain the genetic heritage that drives them to achieve this status in their lives. Their biobehavioral imperatives are on the tips of their tongues. They play to one another and create social institutions—from the dining culture in Los Angeles to the subtleties of the tailoring of their clothes—that allow them to duke it out for top dog using their signs and symbols of wealth, power, and beauty.

FINDING OUR OWN WAY

Needless to say, not all people who have this genetic need to become dominant in order to attract a mate come with the physical attributes that allow them to be that appealing to the opposite sex.

Some of us may try to alter our appearance with different hair styles, eye make-up, styles of clothing, or working out, to enhance or minimize certain of our physical attributes. Eventually however, we run out of tricks and come to accept that we will have trouble competing successfully on our looks alone.

However, who we are is not uni-dimensional. We are constantly presenting different aspects of ourselves to the outside world and receiving feedback. We will pick up feedback from people that let us know what other dimensions of our individuality are viewed as positive by the opposite sex. This behavior goes on between men and women in a complex back and forth pattern of trial and error.

If we are in a social situation and we get a glimmer of interest from a member of the opposite sex in something that we have just said, it serves as the kernel around which we can build a whole persona. Imagine a teenager who receives a compliment from his teacher about the excellent story he has written and then notices a big smile and look from a girl in his class.

Inside his nervous system the bells go off and he feels a sense of pride and a rise in his self-esteem. A dominance battle over all the other boys in that classroom has just been won. The response from the member of the opposite sex tells him that he has an attribute that makes him an attractive mate. The student now knows that he has an ability that puts him in a position of dominance with members of the opposite sex. He may then focus on that activity as one to cultivate. One can easily imagine that choices in careers and personality styles have been made from just such experiences.

The years following puberty are spent in a desperate search for positive feedback from the opposite sex. We may try any one or another activity about which we can brag. Or perhaps it may happen inadvertently that we do something that, much to our surprise, brings a positive response from the opposite sex. The point being that at this time in our lives we are searching for our route, path, or attributes that we have that will allow us to find a hierarchy in which we may achieve a position of dominance and therefore attract a mate.

Once we find that attribute we can then make it a main activity in our lives. It is an area in which we find success and dominance. It is a part of us that allows us to fulfill the primary mission that millions of years of evolution have designed and selected us to achieve—to mate and produce offspring who will carry on and insure the survival of our species.

SEXUAL STEREOTYPES

The breasts of women and the facial hair of men are examples of how men and women differ in a purely biological fashion from each other. This difference is a part of our human genetic heritage, a *fait accompli* in our genes. Women do not learn to grow breasts and men do not learn to grow a beard. One may say that having breasts for women and a beard for men is a typical characteristic that makes a man a man and a woman a woman—a stereotypical characteristic for each gender. If we assume that the kinds of behaviors that we have been describing as unique to men or women are controlled by the biological brain, would it not stand to reason they also could reasonably be considered as sexual stereotypes—biological, genetically inherited traits typical of each gender, with no learning involved.

Another perspective on this very controversial subject of sexuality and stereotypes—the concept of biology as destiny—can be gained from an understanding of one of the fundamental laws of biology and statistics, the bell-shaped curve.

A basic principle of biology is known as *biological variability*. We all know that the typical body temperature of a human being is 98.6 degrees. However, not everyone's temperature is 98.6. Some people are perfectly normal with a bit higher temperature of 99 and others with a bit lower, 98.2. If a study were to be made of all human beings, a graph of how many people had what temperature would appear as shown in Figure 1.

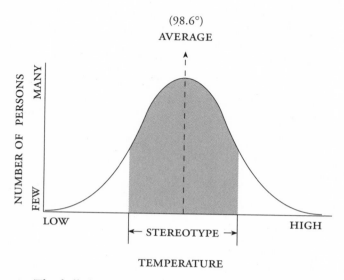

Fig. 1. The bell-shaped curve of biological variability showing the manner of distribution in the population of a biological trait, in this case body temperature.

The average temperature, what could be called statistically the stereotyped human temperature, is 98.6°. The farther away you went from 98.6°, the fewer and fewer people you would find with these nontypical temperatures. This statistical distribution of traits around a central average or stereotypical level is known as biological variability and is common to all things biological. Since the graph of this distribution takes on the appearance of a bell, it has come to be known as the "bell-shaped curve."

GAY REVOLUTION

Not all men have the same density of facial hair nor women the same size breasts. These biological traits are distributed in the manner of the bell-shaped curve. There is a typical amount of male facial hair and a typical female breast size, the central part of the bell. Other men and women have more or less of this trait, and the further away one goes from the stereotype, the fewer people are found that show these statistically "deviant" levels of the trait.

The gay and feminist revolutions are exactly what would be predicted from the biobehavioral imperative theory of human behavior. Most males, whose hormonal values and brain circuitry fall in the large central part of the curve, behave in characteristic ways. That is the reason why we have a male stereotype and similarly one for females. However, as would be expected from the principle of biological variability, there are persons of both genders whose brain circuits and hormones naturally fall outside these typical values. Their biobehavioral imperatives for sexual behaviors are not the typical imperatives. They are not the stereotype. They are the statistically expected standard deviations.

The female imperative to build a nest and to rear children is a stereotypical pattern of female behaviors. However, not all women contain the hormones and brain circuits that control this behavior to the same degree as do other women. Some women are quite happy to take part in the competitive world of business careers and to forego building a nest and rearing children. The same holds true, of course, for men. Not all male teenagers are interested in building their muscles and playing sports. Not all men want to hunt, fish, and spend their weekends rooting for their favorite sports team or working in their woodshops.

There are stereotypical female and male behavior patterns because most women and most men contain the same types and levels of hormones and brain circuits as do other women and men. There are also women and men whose brain circuits and hormones deviate from these typical levels. Their actions are no less under the control of their biology as are the action of other men or women. It is therefore no less imperative that these people also follow the dictates of their biobehavioral imperatives.

A part of our understanding of how the biobehavioral imperatives work also tells us that the *rationale* for a certain lifestyle is just as driven by the imperative as is the life style. It must be appreciated that the philosophical rationale of this, that, or the other liberation or rights movement is driven by the same biological and imperative control systems that caused that person to choose a specific lifestyle in the first place. Therefore, to develop a complex philosophical position as to how women or men should live based upon one's own lifestyle is to do a disservice to other women or men who have different hormones and brain circuits.

As a final comment on the importance of male and female gender roles, I would like to describe for the reader a fascinating paragraph from a book written by a woman who studied chimpanzees. In Stella Brewer's *The Chimps of Mt. Asserik*, she describes her feelings as she lets a chimp that she had helped raise begin to interact with the wild chimps that live around the field station. Stella is of course a female and the chimp she releases is William, a male. She describes her feelings as follows:

> William now eight years old, was clearly adolescent. During the comparatively short time since we had left the reserve, he had steadily shown less need for affection. In Abuko he had looked for excuses to be picked up and cuddled. Now, not only did he refuse to allow anyone to carry him, but he shunned demonstrative affection, turning his face away if he had the slightest suspicion I might plant a kiss on it and firmly disentangling my arms if I gave him the usual good-night hug. I can only interpret his actions and expressions as embarrassment.
>
> I know that a wild chimp of his age would be starting to leave his mother for short periods to travel on the outskirts of all-male groups and gradually introduce himself in the hierarchy. That William was beginning to do the same pleased me, but at the same time I worried slightly. How capable was William of taking care of himself in this new home, which harbored so many more dangers than Abuko? I wasn't sure whether he was aware enough of those dangers to be safe without my protection. Then I shut off those thoughts. He was

with a far more experienced lady than I, a far better teacher, and what we were here for after all.

Tina's swelling [sign of sexual receptiveness] increased that night, and William's interest in her increased with it...

In the above quote we see the fascinating situation of a human mother showing the standard motherly concern in watching her child, in this case a chimp, separate from her care. The male, although admittedly a chimp, is acting no differently than any human male teenager ready to go off in chase of a sexually receptive female, embarrassed at the prospect of a hug and a kiss from Mom. As a result of the genetic heritage we share with our animal ancestors, males are males and females are females whether we are chimps or humans.

AFRAID OF INTIMACY

Mother Nature has chosen women to shoulder the ultimate responsibility for a species' survival. She must raise the child and see to it that the child survives to the age where it can create the next generation. To achieve this goal, a special type of bonding occurs between a mother and a child that is different from any other relationship in the world. The mother also builds a nest wherein she can raise her young. The nest allows her a protected place for breast feeding, a place to keep her child warm, a place for the child to have access to food without competition from other members of the group, and a place for the mother to hide her child from predators. Women bond and nest in all the same senses as do our animal ancestors.

The mother-child relationship is of a different character than other relationships. The intimacy of the relationship between mother and child is what will make the mother defend, care for, and protect the child from all threats. The quality of this bonding may be the basis of one of the more troubling aspects of the relationship between men and women. We have all heard the saying "men are afraid of intimacy." Perhaps men simply do not have the imperative that would lead them to form such intimate relationships as do women. *Men are not afraid of intimacy. The neural circuits of their brains are simply not programmed to participate in relationships in the same manner as are women's brains.*

These same differences in the qualities of relationships between men and women have been described by Shirley Strum in *Almost Human* for male and female baboons as well:

> Such baboon insights are both provocative and complex. Male and female psychologies are already very different among baboons. There is no doubting that females are conservative in trying new behaviors like hunting or in breaking out of old patterns like family rankings; they are unwilling to take risks or strike out on their own. They prefer the safety and reassurance of being with the group and staying close to family and friends. Stability is a goal that they achieve a remarkable amount of the time, sometimes in the face of formidable odds. Males are just the opposite: dynamic risk takers, they seize as many opportunities as they can. If stability and status quo are indeed their goals, these are elusive, at least in male relationships with other males.

THE FORMATIVE YEARS

The biobehavioral imperatives in which we engage as adults begin to emerge during childhood. Our childhood years play a critical role in the development of the skills that allow us to participate successfully in the to-and-fro of the social interactions that have their origins in these biobehavioral imperatives. In animal groups, the young play at the behaviors that are the child's version of the behaviors they will engage in when they become adults. It should come as no surprise that evolution has seen to it that when young we practice those behaviors that will determine the outcomes of our lives as adults and more importantly, the survival of our species. This is particularly true, as it should be for the most critical to our survival of all the biobehavioral imperatives, for sexuality. George Schaller describes just this type of play for gorillas in *The Year of the Gorilla*:

When playing together, the youngsters for the first time in their lives have the opportunity to come into close social contact with each other. Wrestling is a favorite pastime, and usually the arms and legs flail like windmills as the young roll over and over. Another frequent game is follow-the-leader, with the route going up trees, across fallen logs, down lianas, and perhaps across the belly of a dozing female. King-of-the-mountain is played on stumps and in bushes. As one youngster tries to storm the vantage point, the defender kicks the attacker in the face, steps on his hands, and pushes him down. Anything seems to be fair. Yet no one was ever hurt in such games, nor did they ever end in a quarrel.

When by chance a game became too exuberant and rough, an infant showed this by crouching down submissively, arms and legs tucked under, presenting only its broad back to the opponent. An adult female receiving the worst of it in a quarrel with another female may employ the same submissive posture, and the other animal always respects the gesture and refrains from attacking further.

There is great commotion in the twentieth century over the role of learning in developing gender roles. A list of behaviors that seem unambiguously to be more heavily a part of the female gender are nest building, nurturing the young, and using plumage as a sexual attractant, all of which are known without a doubt to be under the control of the brain's biology. Young girls have doll houses and dolls and like to play with lipstick. Young boys play king-of-the-hill to prepare themselves for dominance battles. Is this only because those are behaviors forced upon them by the sex-role expectations of their parents? Clearly not. Their brains and hormones are different. Both male and female children naturally practice those behavior patterns in order to prepare for the behaviors that their adult gender-specific biobehavioral imperatives will force them to perform.

In *The Chimpanzees of Gombe,* Jane Goodall describes some startling sexual behavior of a chimp:

> An extraordinary response to photographs was that of the Temerlins' Lucy. She was given a copy of the magazine Playgirl when she was at the height of estrus. As she came to each picture of a nude male, her excitement visibly increased. She stared at the penis and made sounds similar to those she utters when looking at some delicious morsel, a low guttural uh, uh, uh, uh. She stroked the penis with her forefinger, cautiously at first and then more rapidly. On some pictures she would first stroke the penis with her forefinger, get very excited, and then mutilate it by scratching it with her fingernail. When she finished with one picture she would turn the page and start on another... She did not caress or scratch any other part of the photograph. When she came to the centerfold, she spread it on the floor, positioned herself over it, and rubbed her uvula back and forth on the penis for about twenty seconds. Then she bounced up and down over the penis. Finally, having moved away, she returned and with great care directed a small trickle of urine directly onto the penis.

THE NATURE OF IT ALL

The three biobehavioral imperatives, sexuality, dominance, and territory, have been passed forward to human beings from our animal ancestors. We have now seen how many of the behaviors in which we humans engage and how many of the structures of our human society have their origins in these behaviors. They are as immutable as is our five-fingered human hand and our human heart, a part of our genetic heritage, a part of our humanity.

During my freshman year in college, a professor in a literature course defined literature as *classical* if it dealt with themes of the human comedy and tragedy that are relevant not only to the time period in which the piece was written but also to all periods of human history. He seemed to be equating the themes of classical literature with the essential nature of that which makes us human, whether the action of the literature takes place in the tenth century or the twentieth century. The biobehavioral imperatives are a part of our genetic heritage; they have been with us as long as we have been human. Perhaps this teacher was speaking euphemistically about the interactions between humans that come about because of the role of these biobehavioral imperatives in our behavior.

For example, in the book about Elaine and Willem deKooning "Elaine became a gregarious woman who enjoyed power and dominance...Elaine liked a lot of artists, but only one could be king...Elaine, say friends who remember her early admiration for Bill, was equally determined to be the queen to Bill's king." Biobehavioral imperatives were hard at work in the world of avant garde artists in 1950s New York. When reading Ms. Hall's book, I was not only reminded of a wildlife biologist describing a pack of wolves but also of my freshman English teacher's definition of classical. A long time ago, a very famous writer of classical literature, William Shakespeare, described a similar relationship between a husband and wife. Lady MacBeth, in planning her scheme to make her husband king, said:

> What thou are promis'd—Yet do I fear thy nature:
> It is too full o'th'milk of human kindness,
> To catch the nearest way.
> Thou wouldst be great;
> Art not without ambition, but without
> The illness should attend it:...
> Hie thee hither,
> That I may pour my spirits in thine ear,
> And chastise with the valour of my tongue
> All that impedes thee from the golden round.

LESSON VI
The Animal Prays

Animal societies are organized around the dominant male in whom the subservient members of the group put their faith that he will provide for them and protect them from harm. Similarly, even since our earliest days, we human beings have also put our faith in some form of dominant figure (aka: Supreme Being). We made idols or drew pictures on the walls of caves so that we could worship all-powerful forces such as thunder, lightning, or the sun. Over time, science gradually demystified these forces of nature, yet our brain, thanks to our genetic inheritance from our animal ancestors, still needed an all-powerful figure in whom we could put our faith and trust. Our god genes have driven us to create our modern God. He is the person who is the dominant ruler of our lives. These same genes also contain the blueprint for the behavior that is the universal sign of animal submission to the dominant figure, lowering one's head to the ground in supplication. We have all seen our pet dogs bow to us, their supreme beings. When we humans bow our heads to our supreme being we have chosen to call it prayer. Through our prayers to our supreme being we reduce our anxieties over the uncertainties of our future. Our god genes have driven us to create the concept of religion with its supreme being and our prayers to ask for his help. When we show the universal sign of animal submission and get down on our knees and pray, we may be assured that "God's in his heaven, all's right with the world." Therefore to believe in a supreme being and to kneel before him in prayer is as natural as taking a breath of air, and its psychological benefit to us is every bit as important to our mental well being as the oxygen we breathe is to our body. A belief in a supreme being in whom we can put our faith is the natural Prozac given to us by Mother Nature.

A BIOLOGICAL-GENETIC TRAIT

The similarities between many patterns of human and animal behavior are clear. However, there is one pattern of human behavior that has always been the centerpiece of our thoughts about the uniqueness of humankind. It is our prayers to a god and our faith and our belief in a supreme being who watches over our immortal soul. For the ideas in this book to take on real power, then they must also show that we owe our concept of the God to whom we pray to the animal within us.

One characteristic of a trait that defines it as a biological and an inherited trait is that it is shared by all members of a species. Human beings have always had a hand with five fingers, from the beginning of their existence to the present day. In all corners of the globe, we all have five fingers. No one had to teach us to have five fingers; it is a genetically inherited trait. For a trait to be considered as biological and inherited, it must be present in this pattern, over all time and across all humans in every part of the globe.

No matter where anthropologists have tread, certain behaviors seem universal to our human species. Women decorate their faces to appeal to men, and men show off to appeal to the women. Mothers bond to their children with an intense intimacy, and daughters begin to practice mothering skills with their dolls. Fathers play rough-and-tumble games with sons to begin their development as hunters and warriors. One tribe demarcates its territory and chooses the wisest, biggest, and strongest male to lead the other males in defense of that territory against intrusion by the members of any other tribe. No newspapers, radios, televisions, constitutions, or books by Machiavelli were needed. Human's genetic inheritance made them all act in every corner of the globe in this fashion.

BIOLOGY OF WORSHIP

As is true with these other patterns of behavior, a form of a religion, the worship of a powerful force(s), has also been present in human societies as far back as anthropologists can document our human culture. All primitive cultures that have been studied have made some attempt to create symbols that represent the forces of nature. Whether studying existing primitive tribes that live in remote areas or examining the cave paintings and artifacts of long-extinct primitive cultures, all humans have been found to engage in some form of religion that involved creating symbols, objects that represent the powerful forces, events, or objects of nature. For example, the Maoris of New Zealand worshipped the gods Rongo of the bountiful harvest; Tangaroa, the ocean; and Tane who banishes the darkness. The Aztecs worshipped the gods Xiuhtecuhtli of fire, Tlaloc of rain, and Huaxtec of childbirth; the Egyptian gods were Ra, the sun, Nut, the sky, Osiris of death; and Neit for good hunting. The Greeks worshipped Zeuss the sky god; Poseidon of the sea; and Aphrodite of sexual activity.

Primitive peoples did not know enough about astronomy to know that the sun is an inert celestial body, lighting up their days or putting them into the fearful darkness at night. It was nothing personal, just the laws of physics at work. Similarly, they did not know that the rains were inanimate, not purposefully creating the floods that could drown them or providing the water to quench their thirst and make their crops grow.

Early humans stood in the face of forces that they did not understand nor could they control. At times these forces could kill and at other times provide sustenance. They had a physical presence and impact over life that was of greater importance than the most dominant beast in the jungle. In the face of storms, the moon, and the overwhelming forces of nature, how would the biobehavioral imperatives in primitive peoples react to such threatening, unknown, and seemingly all-powerful forces. The answer lies in the way the biobehavioral imperatives in our animal ancestors respond to dominant forces.

In a fascinating segment from *People of the Forest*, a film by Hugo van Lawick, a thunderstorm occurs and the dominant male chimp replies back to each clap of thunder with his own noisy threat display, beating a branch on the ground. To the dominant chimp's brain, the thunder was a threat display to which he must respond. The chimp's brain, just as for early humans, had no understanding of the true *nature* of these events; they were simply all-powerful and threatening.

Animals have behaviors programmed into their brains that allow them to show submission to a dominant being. Throughout the animal kingdom these behaviors involve some form of lying prone on the ground, such as a dog crawling toward its master. In this way, animals communicate submission to a more powerful being. In his description of studies of wolf behavior, *Dance of the Wolves*, Roger Peters recounts how a wolf responded to a machine that would allow the wolf to touch a bar and then receive food.

> This time, however, instead of pressing, she dropped to her belly, extended her head upward, and frantically licked the end of the bar. She was displaying a posture called active submission, often adopted by pups or low-ranking adults in the presence of their superiors...

The acting out of the submissive posture is also dramatically shown by the following descriptions of chimpanzee behavior, our nearest animal ancestor, in Jane van Lawick-Goodall's *In the Shadow of Man*:

> Just as J.B. looked back she turned to flee; quickly the big male pounded in pursuit, leaped onto her back, and attacked her by stamping with his feet. The female, screaming loudly, escaped, but she only ran a short way and then turned, hurried back to J.B., and crouched in submission until he reached out and repeatedly patted her on the head.

Dr. Goodall describes another example of this submission to a supreme being in her book *Through a Window*:

...Their point made, the brothers sat with bristling hair and looked up into the branches above. Satan, a good deal larger than the new alpha, and in his prime, hastened down and, with loud panting-grunts of submission, pressed his mouth to Figan's thigh. And Figan, utterly relaxed, utterly self-confident, laid a munificent hand on the bowed head before him...

THE GOD GENE

These same supplicant behaviors are a part of our human brain's programs as well, they come wired in as a part of the dominance hierarchy system that we have inherited genetically from our animal ancestors. They are necessary to prohibit the dominant creature from decimating all potential contenders. In describing an early African explorer's account, the African historian Frank McLynn in *Hearts of Darkness* relates a primitive African tribal ritual. A behavior pattern no different than a knight to his King.

His [the King's] people sat on the ground at some distance from his throne; when they approached to address him on any subject they crawled upon their hands and knees to his feet, and touched the ground with their foreheads.

If humans were to be able to quell their anxieties over these all powerful forces that light up the day, make their crops grow, and start fires, then they must show submission to them. In order to do so they would have to create objects—symbols that represent these forces. Early humans' cave paintings and carved idols are the objects they created to stand for, symbolize, these powerful forces so that they could bow down, show submission, and ask them to do no harm and shine their benevolence upon them.

In Marco Polo's diaries he describes the Tartars as "these people are idolaters, and for deities, each person has a tablet fixed up against a high part of the wall of his chamber upon which is written a name that serves to denote the high, celestial, and sublime God...striking their faces against the floor three times they implore from him the blessings of sound intellect and health." Is it an accident that all primitive tribes, even those in the most remote areas of Africa and the Tartars of Asia showed homage by kneeling to their king as did the knights of Europe?

Over time, humans came to understand the moon, rain, thunder, and lightning. Our abilities to control them may still be minimal but at least we now know they are not active creatures, purposefully wreaking their vengeance or beneficence upon us. We have also learned that our prayers will not affect them. So we no longer pray to the gods of the sun and the rain.

However, our lives still have some aspect of happenstance to them, as if there is a mysterious unknown force at work. At times the events in our lives seem out of our control no matter what we do. A loved one dies; a child is crippled in an auto accident, we are laid off at work; an earthquake, tornado, or flood destroys our home; or we try to do our best to achieve a goal but fail. We ask ourselves, "Why? What did I do wrong to deserve this?"

In response to these uncertainties we experience anxiety. We are never sure of the outcomes of our behaviors, nor are we ever sure of what disaster or challenges the fates of tomorrow will bring. We may not know what the force is, but there still seems to be an unseen hand that is affecting our lives in spite of our best efforts to meet our goals and aspirations.

The unseen hand that may be affecting our lives looms over our fates and provokes our brains to show submission and to ask this all-powerful force to spare us from harm. In order to show submission we must create a symbol, a representation, of this unseen force. Once this force that affects our lives is represented in the form of an object, we can then show submission to it and ask for its help no differently than a wolf or a chimp to the dominant male or an earlier human asking the god of rain to quench his thirst. Through our act of submission, we are asking the *supreme being* to make our lives less painful, to protect us, and most importantly, to bless us.

Our brains, under the guidance of our genetic inheritance from our animal ancestors, have created religion, with its deities and prayer, in order to have a way in which we can act out our supplicant behaviors (prayer) to a symbol (God) of the forces that exert control over our lives.

DAILY DEITIES

This very powerful and very human need for the order and structure provided to our lives by a dominant figure is also demonstrated in other cultural institutions that we have created. Most men, at one time or another in their lives, have a hero. Typically this hero is a male who has accomplished great feats of physical prowess. From Mickey Mantle to Michael Jordan, such men have provided the exact figure of a physically powerful male who can give structure, order, and predictability to our lives, just as within any other animal society.

For the female, the dominant leader plays the additional role of a potential mate. Instead of physical prowess alone, females require a component of male sexuality in their choice of a hero. Movie stars and singers, the crooners of old or the rock stars of today, serve the same purpose for females as the athlete serves for the male, with the added component of sexuality. The existence of "groupies," almost always postpuberty females, show just how strong this biobehavioral imperative is.

In primitive tribes the "witch doctor," also known as a shaman, was a powerful figure, a person who held through his mystical powers a position of supreme dominance within the tribe. Although the naturally occurring medicines used by the early witch doctors, or shamans, have in a few cases proven to be valid drugs, the shamans of old as well as the faith healers of today depend heavily upon the powers of faith. It should be no wonder therefore, that "bedside manner" is considered one of an effective physicians most important attributes.

Modern medicine has provided a scientific basis for the mechanism whereby a faith healer can indeed alter the medical state of the supplicant. It is now understood at the molecular level how a person's state of mind can influence his or her health. The brain and the immune system are clearly interconnected via an area of the brain called the hypothalamus. For disorders that have a psychogenic component such as stress or involve the immune system, it is not surprising that a dominant figure in whom patients put total trust and confidence, such as a shaman or a faith healer, would have an impact upon their health.

The importance of our faith in an all-powerful dominant figure for our mental and physical well-being is the reason why we have a cultural tradition in every corner of the globe that the best medicine available to a hurt child is for Mommy or Daddy to kiss it to make it better.

REVOLUTIONARY PROPOSAL

Thanks to our animal ancestors, in our human brain is a program that allows us to feel that we are exerting control over the unseen forces that direct our lives. If we show submission to these forces, we can then hope they will treat us with good will and fortune. So we humans create objects that represent these forces. For most it is called the *supreme being* to whom we supplicate ourselves by lowering ourselves to the ground and praying for his help: "God's in his heaven, all's right with the world." In this way, the biobehavioral imperatives in directing our thoughts and our reasons cause us to create the prayers and gods of our religions.

The revolution of Copernicus, Galileo, and Darwin is now complete. Humankind and its planet earth are in every way truly under the control of Mother Nature. The hand of God moves not in mysterious ways, but in lawful ways, just as the earth moves around the sun, for the hand of God was itself created by a biobehavioral imperative that we inherited from our animal ancestors and that exists in the molecules of our biological brain. The Twenty-Third Psalm may just as easily be the Wolves' Hymn.

GOD'S CREATURES ONE AND ALL

PSALM 23	THE WOLVES' HYMN
THE Lord is my shepherd;	The dominant male is my leader;
I shall not want.	He will provide for me.
He makes me to lie down in	He allows me safe rest;
green pastures;	
He leads me beside still waters	He sees to my safety.
He restores my soul;	He quells my anxiety;
He leads me in the paths of	He shows me how to survive
righteousness	
For His name's sake.	For His name's sake.
Yea, though I walk through the	Yea, though the forest is
valley of the shadow of death	full of threats,
I will fear no evil;	I do not fear them;
For You are with me;	For You are with me;
Your rod and Your staff,	Your strength and Your
they comfort me.	vigor, they comfort me.
You prepare a table before	You protect me from other
me in the presence of	packs;
my enemies;	
You anoint my head with oil;	You bless me;
My cup runs over.	My cup runs over.
Surely goodness and mercy	I feel safe in Your territory
shall follow me	
All the days of my life;	As long as I am in Your pack;
And I will dwell in the	I submit and accept Your
the house of the Lord	dominance
Forever.	Forever.

The Animal Plays

Mother Nature has seen to it that those behaviors that are imperative to our survival give us a feeling of pleasure. That is how Mother Nature guaranteed that we would perform them as often as possible. The most important form of behavior for our survival—reproducing—is also the most pleasurable. If we were not highly motivated to do it, our species would not have survived. Children get tremendous pleasure from playing games. Boys chase around after each other or one type of ball or another. Girls love to play house and mother their dolls. The boys are, of course, practicing the warrior and hunting skills and the girls the nurturant skills that are so necessary for the human species' continuance into the next generation. As children we practice in the form of games these behaviors that are so necessary for our survival as adults. By creating the chemistry for positive reinforcement and associating it with the performance of the biobehavioral imperatives, Mother Nature has seen to it that we will engage in those activities that have provided for the continued survival of our human species.

PLAYING GAMES

As children, most of our time is spent playing, and we do so with great joy. We are either outside playing or inside watching others play on television. When we are youngsters, participating in or watching people play games probably occupies more of our waking time than any other activity and provides us with many of our fondest memories.

As adults, the demands of earning a living shift this balance for it is only a lucky few who can earn a living playing a game. However, our desires to participate have not changed. In fact, there is a great cultural tradition of leaving work early for the golf course, softball field, or ballpark in order to try to shift the balance back to where it was in our childhood. After work we go home and plop down in front of the television to watch sports. Playing and cheering, participating or being a fan, for most, one of lifes greatest pleasures.

We humans who live in complex societies are not alone in our desire to run around playing games. The child in the remote forest of New Guinea chases after the wadded up ball of leaves. The cheetah cub plays with the little mouse and swats at it with his paw. The adult chimpanzee swings from branch to branch in hot pursuit of a rapidly fleeing colobus monkey. Kids in the rain forests of Brazil play the same games as kids connected in cyberspace or even cheetah cubs. A ball or a mouse, a football or a colobus monkey, through all times, across all cultures, and throughout the animal kingdom, kids and adults have one heck of a lot of fun playing at games that involve chasing around after and trying to catch that small, rapidly moving object. How come?

Is spending time chasing after a small object a part of our nature, another of our human behavior patterns inherited from our animal ancestors, encoded in our genes and the neural circuits of our brain? Is the animal within us even in control of our playing sports?

THE BALL AS PREY

Biologists or anthropologists trying to answer this question in a scientific manner would do so by making observations of the distribution of game playing across human societies as well as different animal species. What they would observe is that in fact it is hard to find a human society where the children do not play a game where they chase after a ball-like object. Depending on the society's stage of development, it may be simply a round stone, a wadded up bunch of leaves, or actually a real store-bought ball. If it is a real ball, depending upon the specific locale, it may be a football, hockey puck, baseball, soccer ball, etc.

To the biologist or anthropologist it seems without question that when children chase after a ball, they are engaging in a universal behavior that has been common to all children for all time across the globe. Chasing, after a small quickly moving object is a part of their biological and genetic heritage. A true natural activity. But did we inherit it from our animal ancestors?

We have all seen the kitten batting around a ball of yarn. Those who have watched nature shows on television have seen baby cheetahs, lions, chimpanzees, or virtually any other types of young animals play games where they bound around swatting at a small object. This ball-equivalent is sometimes the tip of Mom's swishing tail, a little rodent, or any other small object that moves around. So playing catch-the-ball games is not only in our human nature but also a part of an animal's nature as well.

Nature is, of course, very efficient and purposeful. The behaviors that twentieth-century humans and animals engage in are not random. They have been finely tuned over millions of years by the evolutionary processes of natural and sexual selection for one very specific purpose: to allow that species to survive and to avoid extinction. Why do kids play chase-the-ball games? The answer is pretty simple: *They are practicing.*

Practicing games helps children develop the skills that will be critical to their survival as adults. Without such programs in their brains, once on their own as adults, they would be inept at catching the prey upon which they feed. Only those animals that contained in their genes the information that caused the nerve cells in their brains to connect together to force the animal to practice and develop this behavior would survive. Proficiency in this prey-catching behavior is necessary in order for the animal to survive and pass on its genes to the next generation. Millions of years of the selection processes of evolution have weeded out those species whose children did not have such a program in their brains.

As adults however, we no longer must hunt to survive. Therefore, our nimble brains have created a variety of substitute activities to allow us to engage in the behaviors for which millions of years of evolution and a childhood of practice have prepared us. Baseball, hockey, or soccer—all forms of chase and catch the small, fast-moving object—are played in every corner of the globe and attest to the biological and evolutionary forces that compel us to play sports. And even if we are not on the field ourselves, we can sit at home on the couch, watch television, and go wild, jumping up and down as our surrogates do the chasing and catching of our next meal for us.

HAVING FUN

We now understand why we play sports so naturally, but the equally important question of why we all get such a kick out of it must also be answered. The answer is in the term "reinforcement," as it is used in the psychological sense. The words "positive and negative reinforcement" are bandied about a great deal in common usage. From the standpoint of the formal, scientific study of behavior, reinforcement is the feedback received by an organism as a result of a specific behavior. Reinforcement influences whether and how frequently the behavior is repeated. A strong positive reinforcement creates a craving to do it again whereas an intense negative reinforcement can cause great reluctance or even a phobia against the behavior.

Who has not seen the joy of a dog that catches a Frisbee and returns it to his owner with an expectant look for the next toss. Clearly the act of catching the frisbee is a positive reinforcement. The dog wants to perform the behavior again. For most of us, there is an undefined joy in "going long" and catching a perfectly timed bomb, in the long run to deep center to make the grab, or the dash down the wing to accept the long pass and deflect it into the net. What an absolute joy. Let's do it again.

A tenet of the behavioral sciences is that positive reinforcers have this property because they are necessary for our survival. Sugar tastes sweet; we want to eat more of it. Sugar is the essential fuel for the body's metabolism. Without sugar's tasting sweet, we would never seek it out as a food with the intensity that is necessary to meet the demands of our metabolism. If we touch something hot or cut ourselves we feel pain, the core negative reinforcer. All activities that occur naturally that are destructive to our biological system and threaten our survival, we experience as unpleasant. Therefore, we avoid them and do not want to repeat the experience.

Mother Nature has seen to it through the evolutionary processes of natural and sexual selection that those activities that we must perform to survive and reproduce as a species are pleasurable and lead to a desire to repeat that behavior. Sex, of course, is the core biobehavioral imperative and is the primary positive reinforcer. Similarly, we experience those things as pain that are destructive to our survival, and we avoid them as much as possible. People never need ask themselves again why they get so much fun out of playing games. It is only as Mother Nature intends us to spend our time.

Cheetah cubs or adult chimps, Little Leaguers, or sand-lot touch football players all seem compelled to chase after that fast-moving little object. Playing sports comes wired into the hard drive of our brain, a part of our genetic heritage. It is fun for everyone because at some time long ago it was a necessary activity for survival. Without it we would have become extinct. So no more guilt about shirking responsibilities when the sun is shining and the call of the ballfield beckons—go for it. Mother Nature wanted it that way.

THE FAN

Whether it is for reasons of age, time, or abilities, as adults much of our involvement with sports is as fans, cheering on our home team. From sports figures endorsing products, team logos on clothing, attendance in person or through a broadcast, there is not an hour in our day that is not touched by some aspect of rooting for the home team. For something to be that much a part of our lives, it must be the expression of some very fundamental biobehavioral needs.

Certainly the importance of learning hunting skills can explain a great deal of our participation in sports when we are children. Sports as a surrogate for the hunting activities that insure our survival can also explain some of our enthusiasm as adults. Yet being a fan, its passion and all pervasiveness in our adult lives, suggests there may be other aspects of our biogenetic inheritance behind it as well.

One additional factor may be sports and being a fan as a way of creating the feelings of self-esteem associated with achieving a position of dominance. We all want to achieve as high a position of dominance as possible, with the territorial and sexual spoils that being king of the hill brings to us. However, a company can have only one president, the club only one golf champion, and there is only one highest house on the hill. The opportunities to be king of the hill are limited.

How then can large numbers of people have the feelings of pride and self-esteem that come from a dominance battle won? Well, what about the New York Yankees? Tens of millions of fans across the country, not just in New York, are Yankee fans. When the Yankees win the World Series, their fans are all kings of the hill. The need to be associated with a winner attracts huge numbers of people to winning teams, and through our fan loyalty we are all dominant for that moment of victory.

In addition to being a fan for a team of many players, we also root for an individual player. For animals and for humans, prior to the development of complex social organizations, the dominant male of one tribe was the guy who went out there and duked it out with the dominant male of the other tribe. The winner's tribe dominated the loser's tribe and took over its territory. Our biobehavioral imperatives want us to have a champion who represents us and through whom we achieve victory over the other side. It is only natural that we have an individual person as a sports hero. We cheer not only for a team, but for a hero, our champion.

BOYS AND GIRLS AT PLAY

Many readers have probably been wondering about sexual differences in our playing and enjoying sports. A fact based analysis would tell us that playing and watching sports is an activity enjoyed primarily by males. Some females play and cheer, with proportionately more cheering than playing, but in the main sports has been a male activity. Most of the really important points put forth in *The Animal within Us* are contained within this set of facts:

First is the notion of the bell-shaped curve and biological variability. A predominance of males over females participates in sports. It could be said that participating in sports fits into the stereotype of being a man. However, some men do not play sports and some women do play sports. This pattern is exactly what would be predicted from a biologically determined behavior pattern, a stereotyped pattern in which most of the gender participates at a certain level whereas as one moves to one side of the curve, fewer and fewer persons participate at the highest intensity levels. On the other side of the curve fewer and fewer participate at the lower intensity level. For women, the stereotype is a minimum of participation and as one moves to either side of this level, fewer and fewer persons are found in the extremes. This is a pattern perfectly fitting the well-known bell-shaped curve of biological variability.

Second, the unequivocal biological determination of these male-female patterns is shown by their presence in the remotest tribes who never read a book or watched television to be taught to act in these male or female stereotypes. Similarly, these patterns of behavior have been constant from the beginnings of recorded history, a part of our genetic heritage inherited from our animal ancestors.

Third is the role of these behavior patterns in the processes of evolution, the survival of the human species. The two necessary events for avoiding extinction are reproduction and sustenance. The female is the reproducer. She carries the egg, incubates the foetus, provides it with its milk, and bonds to it in a do-or-die fashion. As a child she practices those behaviors that are needed to raise the child. She will turn her back on the stick and ball and cuddle the doll. There is no greater joy for a girl than cuddling her doll and playing house. This positive reinforcement makes her practice and hone those skills she will need as an adult if her species is to survive.

Boys are quite a bit different. Running around chasing a ball and play fighting with each other are all practice for those activities of hunting and dominance struggles, the male role in guaranteeing survival. And the fun they have playing these games is positive reinforcement to keep them practicing their adult male skills to ensure the species' survival.

Playing sports and cheering on our home team and our heroes are a part of *The Animal within Us.*

LESSON VIII
The Conscious Animal

It is all well and good to show similarities between patterns of animal and human behavior. Animals, however, are supposed to act on instinct; we humans think and reason before we act. Our human conscious self-awareness is at the core of what makes us unique in the animal kingdom. It is hard to imagine that animals have a conscious, self-aware mind. Yet all that is in our skulls is virtually identical to all that is in their skulls, the same molecules and nerve cells. Could it be that animals also have a consciousness?

The similarities between our human behavior and animal behavior are striking. We have seen the origins for the actions of artists, armies, lovers, worshippers, kings, queens, sports fans, and sports players in the behavior patterns of chimps, wolves, and gorillas. The very core of our humanity, our prayer and our belief in God, is a direct mimic of behavior patterns in animals. All of these human behaviors have their unquestionable origins in the neural circuits of our brain that we have inherited genetically from our animal ancestors.

However, we would all say that animals are acting on instinct. Animals do not read books to learn how to act the way they do, nor do they think about things and then reason out what to do. We humans are not driven by animal instinct; we learn and think and reason to decide what we are going to do. We are consciously self-aware of these thoughts and reasons.

How can we reconcile the parallel between human and animal behaviors with these differences, with the human ability to think and reason? It is a fundamental question that is really another way of asking the basic question of philosophy. What is the nature of our humanity? Nothing would be more important to understanding ourselves than to know the origins of our thoughts and reasons.

Our end-of-the-twentieth-century answer to this question contains two parts. One examines the biological differences that we know exist between the human and animal brain to explain one part of the animal-human conundrum. The second is a novel perspective on our thoughts and reasons that will narrow the gap between our human mind and the animal mind.

UNIQUELY HUMAN BRAIN

There are two major changes that occurred as the human brain evolved out of the brain of our nearest animal ancestors. These two changes are inextricably linked to those aspects of our behavior that separate us from animals and make us uniquely human.

One is that our human brain developed a very large frontal lobe. Our frontal lobe occupies a much larger percentage of our total brain than for any other creature. Through its connections to other parts of the brain, the frontal lobe inhibits and slows down the functions of these other areas. The inhibitory function of the frontal lobe allows humans the ability to *stop and think* before giving an instinctual *reflex* response to a stimulus.

The development of the frontal lobe was the critical evolutionary event for the transition from the relatively primitive social behaviors of animals to the complex and subtle social behaviors of humans. For example, we do not shoot trespassers at will, nor do we launch an immediate attack upon another who threatens our position in the dominance hierarchy. *The inhibitory functions of the human frontal lobe allow us to divert these primitive responses into more socialized patterns of civilized behavior. We stop and think, at least most of us do.*

A famous case in neurology, that of Phineas Gage, shows how the frontal lobe functions and what its loss can mean. Mr. Gage was a well-respected construction foreman for a railroad. In the process of blasting rock to clear a way for tracks, a premature explosion occurred that sent a metal rod up through his eye socket and out the top of his forehead. Although shaken by his injury, Mr. Gage soon recovered and lived for another 13 years, dying in 1861. However, he no longer could hold a steady job. He wandered the country, working here and there, and led a helter-skelter life in contrast to his previous reputation for being a hardworking and trustworthy soul. He now frequently used profanity and was described as seeming to have lost his *moral* way. In the words of his own physician, the damage to Mr. Gage's frontal lobe had altered "the equilibrium or balance, so to speak, between his intellectual faculty and animal propensities." As we will see in Lesson XIII, "The Criminal Animal," the dysfunction of the frontal lobe's regulatory role may be at the core of antisocial and criminal behavior.

As the following joke shows, it is our frontal lobe that makes good poker players of us in the subtle games of human social interactions. A fellow walked into a saloon, stepped up to the bar, and asked for a drink. When he got his drink, he turned to survey the scene. Off in a corner was a table of poker players. Much to his amazement, one of the players was a dog, wearing a green eyeshade and a pile of poker-chips in front of him. The dog was intent on the cards he was holding in his forepaws. The fellow asked the bartender, "Say, is that a dog over there?" The bartender replied, "Yup, sure is. Comes in here every Thursday night, plays a few hands and then leaves." The fellow then said, "That's pretty strange, never seen that before. Is he any good?" The bartender replied, "Not really, whenever he gets a good hand, his tail wags."

If only the dog's brain had a frontal lobe to inhibit his instinctual response to a good hand, it might have been steak every night.

The second main change that occurred as our human brain evolved from that of lower animals was a greatly increased ability to finely control the muscles of our hand and the muscles we use for speech. The areas in the cerebral cortex of our brain that control the muscles for these two functions, hand movement and speech, are greatly expanded in the human brain compared with any other species' brain. As a result, we humans can use our fingers in ways that no other animal can, and we can make a vastly greater repertoire of differentiable sounds than can any other species. Without the ability to finely control our finger movements and our speech, both the written and oral communications systems, speech and writing, that are so essential to our uniquely human mind and its culture, would never have occurred. An interaction between the motivating forces of the biobehavioral imperatives and these two uniquely human features of our brain, created our uniquely human conscious thoughts and our ability to reason.

BIOLOGY OF THOUGHT

We can describe the sensory experience of our thoughts, our conscious self-awareness, in the same terms as the experience we have in our mind when we are talking to ourselves. We hear our thoughts as if we are hearing ourselves speak, even though we are not making any sounds. This experience of a conscious thought is also just like the sense we have when we read silently to ourselves. We seem to *hear* the words even though there really is no sound. Our conscious self-awareness, our thoughts, may be described as the *echo* in our minds of the speech sounds not made.

We can gain insight into the biological origins of these echoes by taking a look at the process whereby we learn to read. As children we are taught to read by mimicking our teachers. We make out loud the same sounds our teacher makes in association with each letter and word. After much out-loud practice we can then read silently to ourselves. When we do so, it is as if we hear in our mind the *echo* of the sound we use to make out loud in association to each letter and word. The echo speech occurs as a result of associative conditioning between the sight of the letter and its associated sound. Associative conditioning holds the key to understanding the thoughts in our mind that constitute our uniquely human conscious self-awareness.

Associative conditioning was described as early as 1872 by the great British biologist-philosopher Thomas Huxley "It may be laid down as a rule, that, if any two mental states be called up together, or in succession, with due frequency and vividness, the subsequent production of the one of them will suffice to call up the other, and that whether we desire it or not." Huxley's idea was eventually proven by direct studies of associative conditioning between nerve cells in the brain.

These studies showed that the natural ability of brain cells to *learn* through associative conditioning is the biological basis for the associative process whereby we learn to read. The repeated association between the visual image of a letter and the sound of the letter causes the brain to eventually hear the sound of the letter in response to seeing the visual image of the letter, even when no sound is actually made.

When we read to ourselves, the associative learning process causes us to internally hear ourselves read.

The process of thinking, whereby we hear our own thoughts, has its roots in the very same associative learning process. Our thoughts are the end result of an associative learning process; we hear ourselves think, just as we hear ourselves read even though no sound is actually made.

Associative conditioning always starts with a pair of events, one of which becomes conditioned to the other. When we learn to read, the initially spoken sound becomes associated to the visual image of a letter. After a conditioning period, the image of letters and words triggers the association, the sound in our mind, even though no words were actually spoken. To understand thought we must find the event inside our brain, that later, because of associative conditioning, occurs alone and creates the *echo* of our speech, our conscious self-awareness, even though we remain silent?

The activation of a biobehavioral imperative in an animal is usually associated with the animal making a sound specific to that imperative. For example, a grizzly makes a specific sound to warn another animal that it has invaded the grizzly's territory. When a grizzly sees an intruder in its territory, it will emit that specific sound to communicate to the intruder that it has invaded the grizzly's territory and that it had better leave or risk an attack.

The same is true for humans. Speech is initiated by our brain in response to signals from either the external world (the sight of a friend) or our body's internal world (hunger). When a newborn is hungry, frightened, or cold, it makes a sound, a relatively undifferentiated sound. As the infant's brain matures, in an uninhibited way and in response to a variety of internal states (hunger, cold, loneliness, etc.) the infant gradually emits more and better-differentiated sounds taught to it by its parents. As these needs and their associated sounds are repeated, associative conditioning takes place, and the sound becomes conditioned to the need. As the child learns a larger vocabulary and the rules of grammar, the sounds become speech. In this way, activation of the whole variety of need states, from hunger, cold, and thirst to the biobehavioral imperatives, becomes associated with the sounds of a complex language.

One of the most important lessons we learn in childhood is when to hold our tongues. Initially, the infant cries, laughs, and coos in an uninhibited way to make its feelings known. During early childhood we are taught that in some situations it is best not to speak out loud. In those situations where we do "hold our tongue" (thanks to the regulatory functions of our frontal lobe), the intention to speak has been triggered, and as a result of previous associative conditioning between the triggering event and the associated sound, in our minds we hear the *echo* of spoken language. We are consciously self-aware of a thought. This sequence is shown in Figure 2.

Our human thoughts, our minds, are the sounds that we have been conditioned to hear in association to the activation of the intention to speak those sounds. Our human self-awareness, the mind of the body-mind duality, is only a singularity and not a duality. *Human conscious self-awareness, our thoughts, can readily be explained in terms of well-known neuropsychological concepts as the echo speech we sense as a result of prior associative conditioning between the intention to speak and the speech sound.*

ANIMAL THOUGHTS

This approach to understanding our own human consciousness presents us with fascinating possibilities about the contents of an animal's mind. For example, what if we were to paralyze the speech muscles of a grizzly? When the *mute* bear sees a trespasser, the biobehavioral imperative to guard its territory will be activated and the bear will try to emit the appropriate "woof" sound to indicate a territorial claim to the intruder just as it previously has time after time. However, for this grizzly no sound will come out. As a result of associative conditioning, will the grizzly's years of woofing at intruders have conditioned it to hear the echo of itself emit the growl?

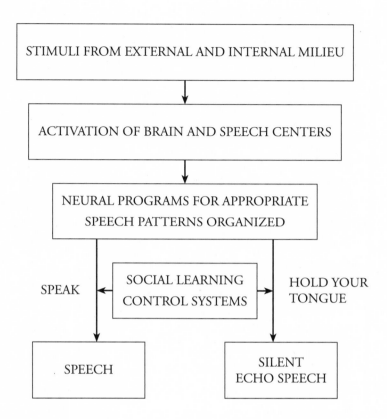

Fig. 2. Illustration of the sequence in the brain whereby a stimulus from either the external or internal milieu gives rise to speech or the silent echo speech we call a conscious thought.

The grizzly sees the intruder and the imperative is activated. The bear's brain tries to emit the sound, but even though no sound is made, the bear's brain hears itself make the sound. Does it have a bear thought? Would the bear now experience what we describe in human terms as conscious self-awareness?

The Conscious Animal Reasons

The biobehavioral imperatives force us to act the way that we do. They are no different from an animal's instinct. Yet we humans would like to think that the decisions we make and the actions we choose to take are carefully thought out, rational decisions, the exercise of our free will. However, the evidence is pretty clear that our reasons are often at the service of biobehavioral predispositions. For example, teenagers, whether a human, lion, wolf, or chimp, under the control of their surging hormones, leave home. In the animal world it is known as "dispersal" and for humans "rebellion." Yet for humans it is accompanied by a complex of intellectualized thoughts which to teenagers are compelling reasons to exercise their free will. This and other similar examples lead us to conclude that much of what passes for human reason and rational thought is labeled as "rational" because it is the chain of ideas that leads us to the behavior already chosen for us by the neural circuits of our brain. The rational decisions we make that determine the course of our lives have their origins in patterns of behavior we have inherited from our animal ancestors.

The regulatory functions of our frontal lobe keep us from giving the instinctual response programmed into our brain by our animal inheritance. Since we have a frontal lobe, we humans can substitute a learned and *reasoned* response. Associative conditioning creates the echo speech that forms the process of conscious thought that occurs prior to giving a response. Our thoughts decide what response we should give. The question remains, what determines the *rationality* of our thoughts? *What is the process that puts our thoughts together into the pattern that we call reason and ends up with a conclusion? An answer to that question, the nature of reason, gets to the very heart of what sets the course of our lives, how we make decisions.*

The question of the nature of reason is a fascinating one. As the old saying goes. "Reasonable people can disagree." Why is it that two people can look at the same set of facts and come to two very different reasoned conclusions. Or in terms of views of the world, to some "The early bird catches the worm" while for others "Haste makes waste." Two people being reasonable but coming to very different conclusions.

When we wake up on the wrong side of the bed, our whole view of the world changes. What may seem a reasonable course of action on that day would be very different from the reasonable course of action when we wake up and feel on top of the world. The facts may be the same, but our reasoned decisions may take us in completely opposite directions. Is there an absolute measure of "reason" or can one person's reason truly be another person's unreasonableness?

THE BIOLOGY OF REASON

When a grizzly bear sees a trespasser and rears up on its hind legs and makes a threat sound, a "woof," it does so at the direction of a biobehavioral imperative. What would happen if the bear had a vocal apparatus that allowed it to make a greater number of highly differentiated sounds and as a cub had learned an extensive vocabulary? The activation of the territorial defense would serve as a trigger for the bear to say to the intruder: "Hey, you can't come in here I have marked the boundaries with my scent. You had better leave." If the bear's vocabulary also contained the word "reason", no doubt he would consider his words the only *reasonable* thing to say.

Another example from the world of animal behavior is a frighteningly exact demonstration of a complex *rational* human behavior with its origins in animal instincts. For most animals, at the time of puberty the young will leave the nest, driven on by a complex interaction of hormones and brain circuits. The teenage lion leaves the warmth and security of the pride and strikes out on its own. He will go far afield to find a territory and a mate to call his own so that he too can produce young who will someday leave home and thus take part in the continuing cycle.

Shirley Strum in *Almost Human, A Journey into the World of Baboons* describes the rebellious angst of two teenage baboons that will surely ring bells for any parent.

> Paul and Sherlock resembled each other in many ways. Both had an intense interest in other troops, assumed a vigilant posture when another group appeared and were among the first to investigate when it came closer. Both remained partially tied to their families while trying to start a different life with other male and female adults. It was Sherlock, though, who had made greater strides along the road that compels an adolescent to leave home. At first he simply moved to the edge of the troop. No one was actually forcing him out; he just seemed to have become a more peripheral member than before. His attention was always elsewhere, always searching for some other troop, in particular the Eburru Cliffs group...
>
> Sherlock wavered back and forth, not just between roles but between troops. I followed. Watching him try to make up his mind was fascinating: one day he would be hovering on

the edge of Pumphouse [Sherlock's home troop] in self-imposed exile, the next he would be wandering off again....Yet the following day he'd take another side trip, this time with a few younger adolescents tagging along in their own peculiar version of an all-male band, Sherlock leading. But what a leader! When the foray ended, Sherlock the Brave rushed back to rejoin Pumphouse, running right into his mother's arms and relaxing for the first time all day.

Whatever the answers, it was apparent to me—and I assume to Sherlock as well—that it would not be easy to go home again.

If we could get into the mind of Sherlock or the teenage lion, what thoughts does the lion or the baboon have about leaving the parents who nurtured them and the security of life with the pride? What type of reasons would they give themselves for "rebelling" against their families?

These animals are playing out a biobehavioral imperative, and so are human teenagers. The conflict of Sherlock between his hormones driving him to leave the Pumphouse troop, yet not quite confident enough to enter the Eburru Cliffs troop, sounds similar to most teenager's ambivalence between leaving the security of home and going out and making their way in the cold, cruel world. What type of reasoned thoughts might Sherlock have used to explain his behavior as he suffered through this stage of his life?

Human teens throughout all cultures and time have felt the same biobehavioral imperative to up and leave the nest, to strike out on their own, often times with the same mixed feelings as did Sherlock. Both Sherlock the baboon and a human teenager behave under the control of a genetically inherited biobehavioral imperative, preprogrammed in the age-related changes that occur in their brains' circuits and hormones; it's their nature. Although changing with the tenor of the times, a host of *reasons* has been put forth for the human teenagers'

rebellion; from the mundane to the complex and deeply philosophical, rebelling and rejecting their families seems only *reasonable*.

Yet at the same time, to their equally intelligent, philosophical,
and perceptive parents, teenage rebellion seems so *unreasonable*. May
one dare to suggest that the rebellion of youth with all its high-minded
justifications is simply a biobehavioral imperative activated by age-
related changes in the levels of certain hormones? Are the time-hon-
ored philosophical underpinnings of rebellion, anti-this, that, or the
other thing, seen as rational because they match with a biologically
driven behavior? Can you imagine if Sherlock the baboon were
human his verbal duels with his parents as he tried to decide whether
to leave home or not, staying away at times but then coming back to
enjoy the security of Mom's touch and protection? Does the old saying "They will grow out of it" have a deeper truth than we imagined?

Teenage rebellion may be explained as a biobehavioral imperative
activated by age-related changes in brain circuits and hormones.
Under the control of this imperative, the human mind then labels the
thoughts that support this behavior as *reason*. This understanding of
teenage rebellion matches perfectly with a famous line from a very
famous movie of the 1950s, *The Wild Ones*. Marlon Brando plays the
dominant male leader of a teenage motorcycle gang. The gang, looking for a territory of its own, has invaded a small town. One of the
townspeople asks Brando "Hey Johnnie, what are you rebelling
against?" Brando responds, "Whaddya got?" In other words, we must
rebel, it is in our genes; any reason will do.

BIOLOGY, REASONS, AND LOGIC

The important role played by the biobehavioral imperatives in
directing our *reasoned* thoughts presents us with an interesting problem. When scientists analyze the results of an experiment, or engineers
make a determination about the structural strength of a bridge, they
use a process of reasoned decision making. Scientists testing the effectiveness of two different drugs find that the number of virus particles
killed by drug A is greater than the number of virus particles killed by

drug B. Therefore logic says that drug A is more efficacious than is drug B. The engineers' bridge must hold the weight of 100 tons. Structural steel type XYZ has that capacity, therefore logic says that steel XYZ will suffice for the bridge. Certainly the logical reasoning behind these decisions is not driven to its conclusion by the biobehavioral imperatives of territory, sexuality, and dominance.

There are two very different types of thinking that we often refer to as *reason*. One is the logical thinking of the scientific method. The other is the perhaps at times illogical but still *reasoned* thoughts that are driven by the biobehavioral imperatives that are focused upon having us behave in a way that will achieve their goals.

The use of the word *logic* in the examples of the scientist and the engineer describes ways of thinking that are reflections of the laws of the physical world. If our tea is too hot, we put an ice cube in the cup to cool it down. Physics has shown that the combination of ice with hot water will lower the temperature of the hot water. A law of the physical world has been used in solving the problems of our daily life. *This pattern of conscious thought known as logical thinking is one where our thoughts follow a sequence that is modeled upon relationships in the physical world.*

For example, when we have a problem to solve, whether it is a cup of tea that is too hot or a dog we wish to train, we look to the laws of nature, the physical world, to find an example of lawful relationships that we can then apply to solve our problem. Just as physics tells us an ice cube will cool the hot tea so does behavioral science tell us a positive reward will reinforce a behavior. So we train our dog by giving it a doggie treat after it performs the correct behavior. In this way we find examples of relationships in the laws of nature that we then apply to solving other problems. It is a form of mimicry, in which we have learned from nature how things work, a pattern of cause and effect, and we then apply these lessons to similar situations. We interchangeably use the words "logic" and "reason" to describe this pattern of conscious thinking.

Our human mimicry of the laws of nature as the basis for our logical thinking is not a uniquely human trait. Mimicry is a behavior pattern that is found extensively throughout the animal kingdom. Observing higher forces at work and patterning our behavior after them is a common feature of our animal ancestors as the following fascinating sequence of chimp behavior described by Stella Brewer in *The Chimps of Mt. Asserik* shows.

It was in one of these tense situations, with Tina sitting in a tree above the kitchen, that I watched William add another item to his growing list of surprises. I was sitting by the fire having a cup of coffee when the chimps came over from the tree where they had been feeding. The kettle was simmering on the fire and instant coffee, sugar and a cup with milk were sitting by the side of the canteen. William wanted my coffee. Looking at Tina, he placed his hand on my cup, slyly glancing back at me. He began to pull gently, continually staring at me. To have a chimp I had raised take advantage of me in this way made me feel really angry. I tightened my hold on my cup, opened my eyes wide and in as deadly a voice as I could muster said: "Willie, don't you dare! Tina or no Tina, I promise you'll be sorry!" Almost immediately his hand and his eyes dropped. I felt he was annoyed, not so much at not getting the coffee as at my unshakable influence over him.

William stalked off to the fireplace. As he leaned over to reach the kettle, his lips curled back in a grimace at the smoke. He touched the handle of the kettle, then drew his hand back. He touched the handle repeatedly, till he found that it was not too hot to hold; then, carrying the kettle carefully and well away from his body, he went to the canteen. In the cup which was already a third filled with milk he placed two spoonfuls of coffee, then four spoonfuls of sugar. Finally he filled the cup to overflowing with scalding water from the kettle. He had my full attention, for the perfectly well-mannered way in which he had made himself a cup of coffee left me speechless.

It was a tin cup and too hot to be lifted, so William crouched over it, making extraordinary faces well before his lips were near enough to suck up any of the coffee. "It's hot, William," I said. "Be careful, it's hot." He glanced at me, his lips still curling away from the heat of the cup. Several times his lips came within millimeters of the hot liquid, but always he drew back before he actually touched it. He was impatient to drink the coffee, but realizing it was still too hot, he spooned some out, bringing the brimming teaspoon to his mouth. Finally he took a quick sip. Though the liquid had cooled considerably, it was still hot enough to make him jerk his head backward and drop the spoon. I expected him to empty the cup in disgust, but he didn't. He looked around, picked up several marbleized stones and dropped them into the coffee. Surely, I thought, he can't know that by dropping cold stones into the cup he's going to cool the coffee? If he realizes that, what else does he know? It was a disquieting thought. Could I have known William intimately all this time yet underestimated him so much?

He placed the spoon in the coffee and stirred it, then tried to sip from the cup again. The temperature just above the surface of his drink told him it was still too hot. He went to the jerry can, took a bulging mouthful of cold water, returned to his cup and spat the water into the cup. It overflowed, and he quickly sipped some of the liquid as it ran over the brim. The coffee was now hot but bearable. He lifted the cup and walked carefully to a shrub just beyond the kitchen; there he leisurely drank his coffee till the cup was empty. I quickly put the sugar and coffee back in the canteen.

ANIMALS, HUMANS, BRAINS, AND MIND

Throughout *The Animal within Us* we have been seeking an answer to the question of how it is that our biological brain creates our conscious, self-aware, and reasoned thoughts. *Our attempt to answer that question has been based upon the form of conscious reasoning known as logic. We have looked to the natural world of animal behavior and the brain's biology for a model, an example, that will then provide us with a logical explanation of our human consciousness and our behavior.* Our search in the natural world has come up with a set of genetically inherited behavior programs, the biobehavioral imperatives of territory, sexuality, and dominance. From these imperatives we have found examples of the type of behaviors that can explain why teenagers rebel in a *reasoned* way that seems so *unreasonable* to others. Or why two people can engage in an argument over a territorial boundary, with each one claiming *reason* on their side.

Here is a review of the logical argument:

First, within the human brain are a set of programs that prompt us to behave in certain ways. These programs focus our behaviors on marking and defending a territory, selecting a mate and insuring our offsprings' survival, and organizing our social groupings into hierarchies. A part of these behavioral programs are vocalizations by which we communicate our needs and desires to others.

Second, human speech differs from animal speech in two ways directly related to the neurobiological differences between the human and the animal brain. Our muscle control center is able to control the muscles we use for vocalization in a much more dexterous fashion than does the muscle control center of the animal brain. Therefore, we are able to make a significantly greater number of sounds than can our animal ancestors. Our frontal lobe is far more developed than it is in our animal ancestor's brain. This frontal lobe has an inhibitory and regulatory function that delays and/or suppresses the reflex vocalization and allows us to replace it with the far more elaborate, complex, and nuance-filled vocalization of human language.

Third, our conscious self-awareness arises out of the process of associative conditioning between the activation of speech and the sounds that our speech makes. Eventually, only the activation of the intention to speak is necessary since it will bring forth an echo of the sounds that we would have made. This *echo speech* forms our consciousness, the awareness of our self.

Fourth, our reason is the chain of thoughts whose conclusion matches with the behavior chosen for us by the biobehavioral imperatives. In this way, the imperatives identify for us which chain of thoughts we will label as reason.

MAKING DECISIONS

When we face a decision, find ourselves in a situation where we must make choices or to take an action our biobehavioral imperatives predispose us to take certain actions. Our human intellect is at the service of these imperatives. The imperatives cause our minds to generate thoughts (echo speech) and to put these thoughts together so that they match in their conclusion the action chosen for us by our behavioral imperatives. It is to that chain of thoughts that we then attach the label "reason", and conversely, a chain of thoughts that would lead to a different action not in keeping with the goals of the biobehavioral imperatives, we label "unreasonable". These instinctual urges serve as the origin of our thoughts, our human consciousness, shaping our language and forcing us to accept as *reasonable* actions that are in reality instinctually driven biobehavioral imperatives. Sometimes we express these thoughts out loud to others. At other times, we keep them to ourselves; they then become the *echo speech* that is the substance of ourselves, our conscious self-awareness.

An interplay of the two types of thought, "logic" and "reason" can be found in a very personal example. As an author I could ask myself a very difficult question. Why did I choose to publish this book? What were my motivations? Were they "logical" or "reasonable"? For more than thirty-five years I have thought about the issues involved in *The Animal within Us*. Experience in writing the results of my research for publication in scholarly journals has taught me the importance and value of writing something down and sending it to colleagues for a critical review as a way to formalize my thoughts and to make sure they are logical and come to scientifically valid conclusions.

I could have written *The Animal within Us* and then shared the manuscript with friends, talked about it, and gone through several revisions to refine the ideas. In this way I would have satisfied the demands and rigor of scientific thinking to make sure my ideas were logically coherent. Once a manuscript was completed I would have been finished.

However, I have chosen to have the manuscript published, receive publicity, and as wide a distribution as possible. Fame and fortune with all their implications for my own position in the dominance hierarchy were at the end of the rainbow. Interestingly, therefore, my own personal biobehavioral imperative of a need to place as high in the dominance hierarchy as possible provided the energy and drive to write, publish, and commercialize these logical thoughts, themselves an attempt to show just how important these imperatives are in driving our human behavior.

The Animal Does Business

We get up every day and spend most of our waking hours engaged in our careers, our business lives. Yet the processes of evolution have shaped the programs in our brains to want us to occupy our time accomplishing the goals of the variety of behaviors essential to our survival, such as defending our territory and establishing our own personal spot in a dominance hierarchy. Is it possible that our 10-hour days, 5 days a week and 50 weeks a year, in pursuit of our careers are really as Mother Nature wanted it? Perhaps having our name on the door or placing photos and drawings on our office cubicle walls really is fulfilling our needs to mark our own territory. Our need for advancement and the power games we play as we climb the corporate ladder may not be all that far removed from the hierarchical struggles within a wolf pack. The money we devote our lives to accumulating we use for the car, clothes, and trappings that show others our hierarchical status. Although it may not seem so at first, yes indeed, we still get up everyday to accomplish the goals of the biobehavioral imperatives as Mother Nature intended, imperatives sublimated into the structure of the daily activities of our business lives.

Not one to leave things to chance, Mother Nature saw to it that our brain evolved with a biological clock to get us up and going each day. We awaken to perform the behaviors that insure our survival. If it were not that way, we human beings would have long ago become extinct. These behaviors are of course the biobehavioral imperatives of territory, sexuality, and dominance hierarchies.

The imperative nature of these behaviors provides useful insight into a question each of us has probably asked. Why do we sleep? A question to which science does not really have an answer. However, if we simply flip the question around, it becomes a no brainer. Why not ask: "Why do we wake up?" Perhaps sleep is the normal idling state of the brain. The active and important part of the sleep-wake cycle is waking up. Evolution and the survival of the fittest saw to it that we wake up to perform the activities of the biobehavioral imperatives, insuring that our species would survive. If our sleep-wake cycle did not have enough time for us to be awake to find a mate and rear our children then we would never have survived as a species.

Back in the old days, some millions of years ago, we humans spent our waking hours protecting our territories and the possessions within them, finding the most desirable partner, mating, and rearing our young, and mostly for the males, vying with each other for the right to perform these activities to insure that our genes were passed on to the next generation.

Some millions of years later we now live within a very complex social system. Civilization with its laws and morals has established formalized methods for protecting our territory and property, getting married, and raising our kids, and for better or worse for the human gene pool, fairly equal opportunity mating. For the past several centuries, our governments, social institutions, and technology have taken care that the goals of the biobehavioral imperatives are fulfilled. However, we are trapped inside our biological brain with its inheritance from our animal ancestors that is still driving us on to act territorially, sexually, and hierarchically. What is it, then, we are to do once we wake up?

THE PURSUIT OF HAPPINESS

Our inventive human brain has created an activity called business and we spend the majority of our waking hours engaged in what we call *business*. *Business is a complex of activities that allows our brain to feel that it is indeed still engaged all day in successfully achieving the goals of the biobehavioral imperatives.* At the core of our business activities is another of our human mind's creations called *money*. Money is the center of the bull's eye toward which our imperatives can direct their aim.

Money is the target at which we aim because it has come to take on the role of a *symbol* and *totem* of territory, possessions, sexuality, and dominance. We get up, go to work, and engage in business in order to earn money. With money we buy a territory and the possessions we hoard within that territory. With money we establish our position within the dominance hierarchy. The things we buy with money allow us to attract the most desirable mate, build a nest, and rear our young in the best way possible. Our thoughts and our reasons under the control of the biobehavioral imperatives have created the activity of business and the symbol of money to allow us to have something to do all day within a culture that has otherwise "civilized" out of existence the pursuit of these imperatives in their primitive form.

Business activities are very complex and civilized. They could not be further from the survival of the fittest battles of the jungle. The rules and regulations of proper business behavior are highly socialized. However, the thoughts and reasons behind even one of the most complex of such business activities, that which is known as a "leveraged buy-out," may not be quite as high level an activity as we once thought. The following description of people and events is based upon a real leveraged buy-out and reveals step-by-step how the biobehavioral imperatives were driving two successful business people to their doom.

The people attending the meeting were at the top of their game. The lawyers and the investment bankers were responsible for most of the important deals of the past decade. The meeting was held in a wood-paneled conference room with a view of the entire city and harbor. The paintings on the wall were mostly scenes of fox hunting among the hedgerows of "jolly olde" England. The signs and symbols of wealth and power were everywhere. John felt good just being in that room, surrounded by those people.

John, however, was an arriviste. This was a different league than he had ever played in before. He at least had the awareness to know the rules of the club so his clothes and social graces fit right in. John's loyal sidekick of fifteen years, Tom, was right there beside him. Tom's clothes and mannerisms did not fit in. He was with John because Tom did know his job, financial analysis. Tom's role was just to sit there quietly and to pass John a note if he heard something he did not like. Tom knew his role well and he put his complete faith and trust in John's skills.

As with such meetings, the first ten minutes were filled with people milling about, getting coffee, returning urgent phone calls. Their behaviors bespoke their importance. People of importance doing important things. The message was loud and clear: do not mess with us, we are men of power.

John looked around at the scene and marvelled that he was a part of it. He had always worked hard and had achieved money, a house in the right neighborhood and all the standard trappings of a success story. John, however, knew there was another level and that he was not, at least until now, a part of it. Masterminding a major leveraged buy-out would put him among the "big dogs," more so than in his wildest dreams.

As with many people who achieve fame and fortune, the start is often a matter of happenstance. At a casual lunch with an old classmate John learned that a major interstate bus company was up for sale.

"They say you are a great warrior."

Drawing by Gahan Wilson; © 1993 The New Yorker Magazine, Inc.

In a matter of months it had progressed from an interesting idea through Tom doing his chief financial officer routine with the numbers, to being here today, surrounded by the legends of corporate finance. John intended to use a leveraged buy-out as a way to own and become chief executive officer of the bus company.

THE DEAL

In a leveraged buy-out, the company's own assets serve as the collateral for loans that provide the cash used to purchase the company. The bus company had been started in the 1920s and included bus depots and their real estate in major downtown areas, which alone formed a sufficient asset base for John to borrow against and raise most of the purchase price. The additional assets, all those buses, provided the basis for additional loans. The willingness of the owners to "share some of the risk" along with John and the banks by taking some notes and equity in lieu of cash made the whole deal come together.

Tom certainly had done the number crunching and the message was obvious. Operating earnings would just barely generate the cash flow to cover this mixture of debts. Interstate bus travel was not exactly on the upswing. The slightest hiccup and the debt service could not be paid. Anyone who knew these facts could become very nervous about the whole transaction.

Indeed, it all did make Tom very nervous, and he had told John so. The story behind the numbers was inescapable. Yes, the asset base could be used to borrow a big chunk of money to buy out the previous owners. The company's minimal operating earnings were a mixed blessing. They were low enough to allow even an optimistic multiple-of-earnings calculation to produce a buy-out price small enough that it could be met mostly with the cash raised through debt. On the other hand, the same low earnings that gave the minimal purchase price also would generate a minimum cash flow so that servicing the debt was such a close call. The financial analysis showed John and Tom they were on a very fine edge.

DREAMS OF DOMINANCE

Tom laid out all of the numbers and showed John how vulnerable they were. John however was filled with optimism. He had plans. New programs to increase ridership. Expenses could be cut. Interest rates were sure to head down, not up, giving an even larger debt-service cushion.

John however, wanted to do the deal. He could imagine the article in *The Wall Street Journal* when the deal was announced. He would go to the head of the class, the big time. These thoughts came to him as he looked around the room. He would be not just another successful businessman, but now a major player in the arena of big-time deals.

The lawyers and the investment bankers were the big leagues and now he was a part of it. In fact, they were all here today because of him. It was *his* deal. Tom's number-crunching concerns were the last thing on his mind. After several days of last-minute negotiating and initialed changes to signed documents, the deal was done. John's deal was done. He did it. He made it happen. John was now a national figure in the big leagues. God he felt great.

LOGIC INTRUDES

Fast forward five years. John and Tom sat at the conference room table looking at the numbers, summaries and detailed line items to support them that told an ugly story of deep trouble. The worst had happened. The interest rates on the debt had floated up and the ridership had gone down. There was no way in hell they were going to be able to service the debt. They could stay alive for four more months. All the actions they could think of had been taken, to no avail.

Tom knew it was not a time to say "I told you so." That was not his place. However, he had in fact told John so five years ago. Now even John could not ignore the numbers. It was 9:00 *p.m.*; they had been at it all day. John told Tom they had to face the facts and decide how to put an end to it. An asset liquidation sale, a workout under a bankruptcy proceeding, or just do one of those change your name and disappear routines,—what the hell. It was time to go home. That the end had come was now clear. Tom could not help but think that it was clear to him five years ago that this day would come eventually.

During the drive home, John reminded himself that he had always taken pride in his own analytical abilities. How the hell had he gotten himself into this mess? What could he have been thinking about five years ago that made him get involved in something so risky? The cash-flow analysis had been there for all to see. How could he have deluded himself into thinking that it would work? What a fool he had been?

Tom, during his drive home, was also very upset. That a catastrophe was just waiting to happen was as clear to him five years ago as it was today now that the catastrophe was upon them. Now he, Tom, would be forever thought of as the chief financial officer of one of the biggest deals to go bust in recent history. How had he ever been a part of this, much less let John go ahead with it?

THE ANIMAL STRIKES

The Animal within Us has been building a logical argument that our most intellectualized of human activities and the thoughts and reasons we have for those activities have at their roots a group of biobehavioral imperatives hard-wired in our brains, which we have inherited from our animal ancestors. We humans are at the mercy of the behavior patterns inherited from our animal ancestors, in spite of the depth and complexity of our human culture. Could one of the most sophisticated of business transactions, a leveraged buy-out, done by two seasoned and successful business executives, really be just a sublimation of the drive provided by these imperatives? Were Tom and John just animals expressing these survival-of-the-fittest behaviors in the twentieth-century human jungle?

From the perspective of *The Animal within Us*, the decisions and actions of both John and Tom can be readily understood. In fact, if both our deal makers had been sensitive to the interactions between their thought processes, decision making, and their own biobehavioral imperatives, they may have been saved a lot of grief.

For example, as described in Lesson IX, we know that humans engage in two types of thinking. One is logic, thought sequences patterned after the laws governing the physical world. When we add up the costs of a vacation, if the sum is greater than the amount in our budget, we logically conclude we had better try another trip. The second is reason, thought patterns that are driven to conclusion under the control of the biobehavioral imperatives. When we are shopping for a new house and find two houses that are equal in every respect except for price and neighborhood, we will reason our way to paying more for a house in the fancier neighborhood, thrusting out our chest each time we tell someone where we live.

How about for John and Tom? Were they acting under the guidance of logic or of reason? Logical thinking clearly showed how unlikely it was that the cash flow would cover the debt payments. If John and Tom had thought only logically, they would never have done the deal and would have saved themselves five years of trouble. But they did not. Why not?

TOM'S ANIMAL

For the past fifteen years Tom had followed John's rising star. As a result of biological variability, Tom's brain circuitry did not demand that he always be the dominant male. Tom's place in the sun was as number-two man to John. He was satisfied with the reflected glory and all it brought him.

If Tom had relied on his expertise in financial analysis, his decision on the leveraged buy-out would have been logically clear: no go, too risky. However, at some unconscious level Tom understood that his place in the sun was dependent on following John. The logic of the numbers in the financial analysis was no match for the force of Mother Nature driving his conscious reasoning to make a decision that would maintain his position in the hierarchy. His unconscious was all too aware of the consequences of challenging the dominant male. Tom would never tell John he would have nothing to do with this foolish enterprise.

JOHN'S ANIMAL

John, on the other hand, always had to be the best. If he started something and saw he would not be the best, he quickly dropped it and tried his hand at something else. His wife had dreams; she shared John's ambitions. As John's business career found success, at each step they moved to a fancier house and car. However, he and his wife still lusted after the bigger castle on top of the higher hill.

Within the business community the hot people were not just making money, but doing so in a cutting-edge type of transaction. The men were separated from the boys by not only how much money you made but how you made it. To John, a megabuck leveraged buy-out sure sounded better than selling hot dogs at baseball games, no matter how many stadiums you controlled and how big was the bottom line. A big-buck leveraged buy-out and the biggest castle on the biggest hill were soon to be his. He and his wife could strut their stuff in Aspen with the best of them. His wife might even be asked to join the board of the art museum and the opera. During the time the buy-out was in negotiation, John and his wife salivated each night as they imagined the fame and fortune that lay ahead.

So he had done it, gone ahead with the deal. Tom had raised some cautions but not too vociferously. But now, five years later, John was humiliated. He had grabbed for the brass ring and fallen off his horse. His wife no longer went to the club; she was embarrassed by the failure of her husband. John did not know what to do. How could he ever find a way to pay for the mortgage, the car, the private schools for the kids, or the condo in Aspen. He felt utter despair.

During the time I was writing this book, I read *Hit and Run: How Jon Peters and Peter Guber Took Sony for a Ride in Hollywood* by Nancy Griffin and Kim Masters. Just as with the book on DeKooning, or Herodutus' *Histories*, Griffin's book might as well have been a wildlife biologist describing a wolf pack. It describes a business duo just like John and Tom, one dominant and the other submissive, and each all too willing to play their role. The authors write: "Jon knew that Mark Canton would remain his loyal slave if he rose in the studio hierarchy—Canton was easily dominated.—He was like an obsequious little brother, timid and unimpeachably loyal."

SELF-KNOWLEDGE FOR A BETTER TOMORROW

Following their last meeting, John and Tom had a great deal to think about. They were each a bit baffled by just how completely things had fallen apart. Fortunately John heard about a book called *The Animal within Us.* He read the book and started thinking back to the pattern of his life: how he always had to be the best. His career had jumped from one activity to another; he really did not care what he did. He was only looking for a train to ride to the top of the hill. When the ride slowed down or seemed headed down hill he bought another ticket and rode another train. His wife was always so supportive of what he did; he felt lucky in that regard. Now he wondered, perhaps her support was simply so she too could arrive at the top of the hill.

These revelations were mind boggling. John asked himself what had he done simply because he enjoyed the activity for itself? It seemed that his thirty-year business career had been directed simply at providing his wife and himself with a house on a higher hill so he could look down on more and more houses on lower hills and up at fewer and fewer houses on higher hills. Thanks to his understanding of these motivations, his despair was beginning to lift; he needed to spend some time figuring out what he really enjoyed doing and then have a long talk with his wife about the new life he planned to start.

Since their last meeting, John and Tom had barely spoken other than about what had to be done to put the bus company to bed such as selling the buses and the routes to another company and turning over the real estate to the bank. John put his copy of *The Animal within Us* in the car and headed out to give it to Tom.

A week later Tom finished the book, turned off the reading light, snuggled next to his wife, and closed his eyes. Some thoughts began to come to him that he had oftentimes sensed were on his mind, but he had never really stopped to think about them. He had often overheard the snickers from others in the office about his being a "yesman" to John. If John asked him to jump, Tom's response was "how high?" Was Tom simply a member of the pack, totally subservient to the dominant male, John.

Tom awoke covered with sweat; the dream that woke him was still in his mind. There was a pack of wolves; one of the subservient males challenged the dominant male. This wolf had made a few half-hearted challenges in the past, but always backed down. This time he planned to make it stick. Both wolves had their full snarl on. Stiff legged they moved around one another, the hair on their backs standing straight up. The dominant male made a few feints toward his challenger. The challenger stood his ground. He would not back off. The dominant male leaped up with teeth bared and zeroed in for the final attack. The subservient male woke up. Tom was covered with sweat. As he tried to fall back asleep it became clear to Tom what he had to tell John the first thing in the morning.

As described by R.D. Lawrence in *In Praise of Wolves*, and as happened for Tom in his dream, the border between the animal and human mind and feelings may not be as clear as we usually think.

> During these nights, I would often go outside, enter the enclosure, and squat in the snow, flanked by the wolves. Silently, communicating through body contact, we would watch the red-green stars and the coruscating aurora borealis and we would become as one under the blazing heavens. Sometimes I would be compelled to howl; and even as I prepared to do so, Tundra and Taiga would be equally urged, their ululating songs rising above my puny voice and echoing throughout the wilderness.

The Pack Attacks

One hates to say it, but war is only natural. Fortunately, so is peace. Both behavior patterns are common to every form of animal. Struggles over claims to territories and establishing a position as leader of the pack are at the origins of our animal ancestors battle's. Since we have inherited these patterns of behavior from our animal ancestors, it should come as no surprise that our human killing fields are spawned by the same drives. From an understanding of the true imperative nature of waging war and what it takes to switch over to waging peace, we can find more effective ways to control this most destructive aspect of our animal inheritance.

Under the banner of a territorial group we humans have managed to create the largest killing fields known in the history of the animal kingdom. When one group decides to take over another group's territory, we kill each other off in the millions. However, it is not just the biobehavioral imperative of territory that drives us to perform these deeds, but the imperative of dominance as well. These imperatives not only drive us to kill but also provide the *echo speech* rationale for our biologically driven behavior: "My country right or wrong." Interestingly, however, as we shall come to see, the biobehavioral imperatives are also the source of the institutions and reasoned thoughts that we use to bring about peace.

To understand how the biobehavioral imperatives cause human beings to wage war and peace, we can start with a simple human territorial group such as a tribe. A tribe is ruled by a dominant male, called a king or chief, who selects a female as his queen. They rule over a defined territory.

Within the tribe's territory are numerous other families, each one of which marks off its own territory. Within its own territory each family keeps its possessions. The quantity and quality of these possessions sets the basic ranking of that family within the tribe's hierarchy. The king, of course, has the grandest possessions, and depending on his authority may even have the right to tax the less dominant members of the tribe so that he may add to his store of possessions. He also has the main responsibility for overseeing the maintenance of the tribe's territory, protecting its resources and its inhabitants from competing tribes. This tribal structure is little different from the structure of a lion's pride or a chimp's troop.

In these ways, the imperatives of territoriality, dominance, and sexuality set the organizational structure and the internal rules by which the tribe lives. The more modern social structures of cities, states, and nations, are little different from the primitive human's tribe, but since they contain so many more people there are simply more layers of organization.

TERRITORY: A MATTER OF LIFE OR DEATH

Virtually every war has been fought over a territorial dispute. The origins of these disputes are several. One is the resources in a tribe's territory. When a tribe's population outgrows the natural resources within its territory, the tribe must expand its territory in order to provide food for its people. Or, if a natural occurrence such as a fire, flood, or drought causes a famine, the tribe must expand its territory to feed its people.

If a tribe wishes to expand its territory in order to have access to additional resources, it must take control of a territory already claimed by another tribe. These other tribes are probably experiencing stresses and strains on their own resources or remember time periods when that was the case. Therefore, they would not be willing to just give up their precious territory to another tribe.

For the members of one tribe to survive, they must take by force the territory necessary for their tribe's survival. Led by their dominant male, they wage war; their survival is at stake. Remember, to accomplish the goals of the biobehavioral imperatives is just as imperative to our brain as is keeping our heart beating.

We humans did not have to read a book to know that we must defend to the death the resources in our territory. As shown by R.D. Lawrence in *In Praise of Wolves*, this behavior is a part of our genetic inheritance.

The fact that Isle Royale wolves literally went to war in response to the stress created by their overpopulation, which is something that these animals have never been known to do before, is in itself of the greatest importance to all those who are concerned about man's penchant for killing his own kind.

There is no doubt at all in my mind that the Isle Royale wolves warred on each other because of overpopulation, food shortages, stress, and their inability to disperse, as their kind will do in mainland habitats when faced by the same problems.

EMPIRE BUILDERS

Wars over territories may at times be completely independent of such a *rational* reason as obtaining food to avoid starvation. They may simply come from the hierarchical madness inherent in the neural circuits of the dominant male's brain. The fact that an individual fights his way to the top, becomes chief, and takes on the responsibilities of the dominant male indicates that he is at the extreme of biological variability in his need for dominance. He is a victim of his nervous system; it is his nature. His dominance drive may be sufficiently strong that the leader wants to expand the territory over which he is lord and master and take another tribe's territory simply to extend his reign and increase the territory and possessions over which he may lay claim. The term "empire builder" has come into common usage to describe the dominant male who seems to want to be lord and master over something, business or territory, purely for the sake of expanding his sphere of control.

REVOLUTIONARIES

The dominant male of a tribe is not only at risk from challenges by another tribe, but also the challenge may come from within his own tribe. Such internal challenges are an everpresent fact of life for the dominant male. In his own tribe there is a constant supply of young males passing through that age when their own hormones and brain circuits are driving them to find their own place in the hierarchy.

For those on the extreme of the bell-shaped curve, king of the hill is the only place acceptable. The challenger must then instigate a revolution to overthrow his own tribe's current king. Such revolutionaries, depending on circumstances, have several ways to depose the current ruler.

If the tribe's tradition calls for a one-on-one battle, he will make his intentions known and duke it out with the king for control of the tribe. Or he may recruit other young bucks to his side, and with an overwhelming display of might, force the current king to capitulate his throne.

If the revolutionary fails he must, just as in a lion's pride or a chimp's troop, leave his territory and find acceptance in another tribe's territory. In our human world, we use the term "exile." Once in exile he may affiliate with another tribe and its powerful ruler and then use the strength and power of his new allies to attack his former tribe in another attempt to gain the dominant position. Such a strategy may also be used by a deposed ruler to reassert his previous position of dominance. None of which is very far removed from our animal ancestors as described by Jane Goodall in *The Chimpanzees of Gombe.*

The two big males fight, rolling over, grappling and hitting each other. It is not until the battle is already in progress that we realize why Goliath, so fearful the evening before, is suddenly so brave today: we hear the deep pant-hoots of David Greybeard. He appears from the undergrowth and displays in his slow magnificent way around the combatants. He must have joined Goliath late the evening before and even though he does not actually join the fight, his presence provides moral support.

Can the origins of our human history of war be summarized so succinctly as in the previous few pages? Can it really be that simple? There is not a war in human history that does not fit one of these patterns. The biobehavioral imperatives of territory and dominance are as basic, immutable, and powerful as the laws of physics that cause the earth to move around the sun. They drive us to kill as a way of defending our territories and our status, all the while creating the thoughts and reasons that are needed to intellectually justify our killing millions of our fellow humans.

There could never be a better example of the *illogical* yet *rational* decision by a leader to maintain his status at the cost of his countrymen's lives than the dropping of the second nuclear bomb over

Nagasaki in 1945. The first bomb used against Hiroshima made a compelling, *logical* case for Japan's surrender, yet because of its' rulers nationalistic pride, *reasons* came to mind to justify not surrendering. Boom, an additional tens of thousands dead.

ALLEGIANCE

A fascinating question that arises when trying to view our human wars within the context of the biobehavioral imperatives is the level of our territorial affiliation. Do we go to war for our family, our tribe, our city, our state, or our nation? At what level of social organization are we prepared to lay down our lives? "My _____ right or wrong"—what is the correct social/territorial grouping to use to fill in the blank?

Today, in the Middle East, Africa, or eastern Europe, we have tribes/clans fighting for the lands occupied by their peoples for generation after generation, going back thousands of years and in some cases, perhaps even as far back as the early evolution of humankind itself. The recent spate of such conflicts in Somalia, Rwanda, and Bosnia as well as the Arab-Israeli struggles go back hundreds and thousands of years, and reflect the genetically inherited ritual of tribal/clan social groupings defending to the death their territorial homeland. The original Americans, American Indians, laid down their lives in the face of overwhelming force to defend their tribal homelands.

In all of these cases, Africa, the Middle East, eastern Europe, and North America, a variety of tribal and ethnic groups were forced to live within territorial boundaries that were not based upon ethnic homelands but drawn for geographic or strategic reasons by colonial powers. Any attempt to create a city, state, or nation, that does not give recognition to this most primitive of affiliations is in the long run doomed to failure. Just as the spider had to be bite the frog, so too must a clan defend its ancestral home, it is their nature. In *Through a Window*, Jane Goodall describes for us how our nearest animal ancestors, chimpanzees, with whom we share 99% of our DNA protect the land of their birth. A description we should keep in mind as the super-powers reorganize the territorial boundaries of others.

1974 marked the start of "the four-year war" at Gombe. Ten years after I arrived at Gombe, the community whose members I had come to know so well began to divide...the brothers Hugh and Charlie and my old friend Goliath, began to spend more and more time in the southern part of the community range. Sniff, who was an adolescent at the time, and three adult females with their young, also became part of what we called the "southern sub-group." The "northern sub-group" was much larger, with eight adult males, twelve females and their young...

When males of the two communities encountered one another in the overlap zone between the two, they typically hurled noisy insults at each other, displayed long and vigorously, then retreated, each side back into the safe heartland of its own newly demarcated territory...

...and then came the first brutal attack by Kasakela males on a Kahama male.... Figan, Jomeo, Sherry, and Evered pounded and stamped on their victim, while Humphrey pinned him to the ground, sitting on his head and holding his legs with both hands. Godi had no chance to escape, no chance to defend himself. Rodolf, the oldest of the Kasakela males, hit and bit at the hapless victim whenever he saw an opening and Gigi, who was also present, charged back and forth around the melee [perhaps the chimp analog of the female cheerleader on the sidelines]. All the chimpanzees were screaming loudly, Godi in terror and pain, the aggressors in a state of enraged frenzy...

Over the next four years, four more assaults of this sort were witnessed. The second victim was the young male De. He was equally badly wounded as a result of a twenty-minute battering inflicted by Jomeo, Sherry and Evered...

Willy Wally was the next to vanish. And then, for a year, Sniff was the lone survivor of the Kahama males, confined to a tiny area sandwiched between the Kasakela community to the north and the powerful Kalande community further to the south....

But Sniff was brutally murdered like the others. Hunted down, attacked and left incapacitated, bleeding from innumerable wounds and with a broken leg. Once again we all went out to search for him: once again we failed to locate the place where he had crept away to die. His passing marked the end of the Kahama community.

PREDESTINED TO WAR

Our behavior, so we humans would claim, is a result of our thoughts and reasons, not just a preprogrammed instinct as are the territorial and dominance wars of wolves and chimps. However, we have inherited from our animal ancestors these very same instincts in the form of the biobehavioral imperatives. They shape our thoughts and construct our reasons so that we ultimately perform, in a human-derived form, the instinctual behavior programmed for us in our biobehavioral imperatives. The control by these imperatives of our thoughts and reasons and the human social institutions that they create is never so apparent as it is in why we humans go to war. We go to war to inflict death on others and possibly to suffer the same fate ourselves, even to the point of forcing a nuclear holocaust, under the completely *illogical* but otherwise *rational* saying: "My country (territory) right or wrong." At the risk of sounding extraordinarily cynical, war is only natural.

PREDESTINED TO PEACE

Understanding the origins of wars in our animal ancestors has provided us with insight into the origins of human conflicts. It is important to realize that our animal ancestors are also pretty skilled at waging peace. An understanding of the animal's methods of peace

negotiations, such as the following described by Vitus Droscher in
They Love and Kill may provide us with a similarly valuable insight
into how we humans can also go about waging peace.

> The gibbon neighbors work off their aggression by
> singing at each other for half an hour. Then all the gibbons
> grow calmer, and neighbors eye each other with hostility
> through the leaves. At this time, young gibbons from enemy
> territories are allowed to play together...

Not just for gibbons but for virtually all animal species, territorial disputes are typically settled before the combat becomes fatal. At
some point in the struggle, one of the combatants will perform a submissive display to the other, and the combat is broken off. Not unlike
the animals, we humans also engage in complex ritualized behaviors
that allow us to settle territorial disputes short of a killing war.

We have created an institution known as the United Nations as
the arena whereby the leaders (typically the dominant males) of the
various nations (territories) meet in verbal combat to settle international disputes. It is a tribute to our inhibitory frontal lobe and our
fine control over the muscles of vocalization that we have been able
to create an institution as complex, subtle, and sophisticated as the
United Nations out of the biobehavioral imperative for resolving territorial disputes.

At the United Nations, the leaders of the pack (or a surrogate)
from each nation, face off against one another and through the use of
a variety of communications both verbal and body language, engage
in a long drawn-out duel for dominance. At times, leaders will gang
up and form alliances, and just as in the example of the chimp presented earlier in this lesson, the leader from a lower-ranking country
may prevail because of his affiliation with the leader of a more dominant country. Through this give and take, ebb and flow, power is
displayed and eventually one side or the other prevails and in that
mysterious process whereby the communication signals do their
work, just as for the gibbons, one side decides to submit to the other.

In one of the more memorable moments in United Nations history, when human language failed him, Nikita Khrushchev took off his shoe and pounded it on the table, just as the dominant male leader of a troop of chimps would have done with a branch. As the old saying goes, "The tune remains the same, only the words have changed."

After all, it may be one nation with millions of people against another nation with millions of people, but when it comes down to it, the supreme leader of one tribe sits across the negotiating table from the supreme leader of another tribe, both of whom possess biobehavioral imperatives that drive their thoughts and reasons, with the lives of their millions of constituents hanging in the balance. Perhaps, from an appreciation of the role of these imperatives in war and peace, we may find more effective ways to prevent war, and if already engaged, to bring it to a safe and rapid conclusion.

The Dysfunctional Animal

If the biobehavioral imperatives are truly at the origins of our thoughts and feelings, then they should also be at the origins of the disordered thoughts and feelings of the mentally ill as well. Indeed, examples of disturbed behavior patterns that mimic forms of human mental illness can be found in animals. Understanding the relationship between accomplishing the goals of the biobehavioral imperatives and mental illness sheds important new light into the working of the mentally ill mind. Such insight could be at the basis of a new form of therapy, a biobehavioral therapy. Understanding one's psychic pain from this perspective should alleviate that pain and focus one's activities into psychologically productive channels. We must learn how to make the animal within us wag its tail as often as possible.

The most common types of mental anguish suffered by humans are the intrapsychic pain of anxiety and depression. Whether it is the mild form of anxiety and depression that all people experience now and then, or the true clinical depression and debilitating anxiety with loss of appetite, sleep disorder, and other paralyzing behavioral symptoms, anxiety and depression have been experienced at some time in our lives by virtually all of us.

The origins of our human anxiety and depression are not hard to find. A variety of anxiety- and depression-like episodes have been described for animals in their natural settings. An example is Vits Droscher's description of a depressed gnu in *They Love and Kill*:

> Thus the possession or loss of territory has a profound emotional effect on a gnu. Being master of a small strip of grassy plain gives a male gnu a feeling of self-confidence and superiority to other gnus. When a bachelor acquires property, his inferiority complex disappears, allowing his natural aggressiveness and sexuality to reassert themselves. If he loses his land, the result is "psychological castration."
>
> Thus the ownership of territory is mostly a state of mind. Without territory, no male gnu can reproduce.
>
> With a few unhappy exceptions, the defeated bull does not lose his life but only his property and self-esteem. He now has no choice but to remain a bachelor or to undertake the laborious task of insinuating himself into a new territory.
>
> The talent for acquiring territory varies from bull to bull. Some bulls can acquire it in a few hours; others take weeks; still others fail altogether.

Jane Goodall in *Through a Window* empathizes with a chimp who has just lost a battle for dominance, a sure candidate for an antidepressant.

A week after his defeat, I followed the fallen monarch when he left camp. He moved slowly, pausing often to pick and munch on various leaves and fruits along the way. Later, in the heat of midday, he bent a few saplings onto the ground and settled down on this little bed to rest. I leaned against the trunk of a gnarled old fig nearby. It was quiet and very peaceful. Mike lay, his eyes open, staring into space. As I watched him I wondered what was going on his mind. Was he regretting his lost power? Is it only we humans, with our constant preoccupation with self-image, who know the crippling sense of humiliation? Mike turned his head and looked at me, looked directly into my eyes. His gaze seemed untroubled, serene. Perhaps, I thought, he was glad to relax and let go the reins of power. After all, it is hard work for a top-ranking chimpanzee to maintain his position even when he is strong and young. And Mike was old, so tired. Presently he closed his eyes and slept. Later, when he awoke, he wandered off into the forest, a solitary figure, very small under the huge trees.

Humphrey automatically succeeded Mike as alpha...

The naturalist and explorer Jean-Pierre Hallet writes in his book *Animal Kitabu,*

Without a territory to defend, without a strong central focus for continuing existence, animals of greatly varied species will grow listless and indifferent.

These descriptions show that for animals there is a relationship between the animals success in achieving the goal of a biobehavioral imperative and a behavior very similar to the anxiety and depression experienced by humans. When we humans lose a battle for territory, dominance, or attracting a mate, how does our brain respond? Is the frustration and failure to achieve a biobehavioral imperative experienced by the human psyche as anxiety and depression?

Our actions every day are driven/motivated by our biobehavioral imperatives. Whether we are trying to achieve a position of dominance or find a willing mate, we are acting out imperatives. Our brain drives us on to achieve their goals. When we meet with obstacles we try even harder, searching further for a mate, or working longer hours on our job. The more frustration we experience, the harder we try. All along the way we begin to feel a state of anxiety that becomes more and more intense the more frustrated we are in fulfilling the imperative. As we begin to run out of choices to achieve our goals and the prospect of failure becomes real, the anxiety converts into depression. *Anxiety and depression are the brain's response to our failure to achieve the goals set for us by biobehavioral imperatives; the anxiety evolves into depression as we become more frustrated in achieving those goals and our failure appears more absolute.*

PSYCHOSES

Depressed and anxious people can feed, dress, and house themselves. They are certainly not very happy, and it may be with a sense of gloom, but they do go about the daily basics of living. Psychotic individuals however, live in a world where there is a complete break with reality. They hear voices and have visual hallucinations. The reality shared by most of us is not theirs. Theirs is a world of fantasy.

A psychotic is that way because the chemistry of their brain is very different from a normal person's. The details are unknown; if they were known it could be easily fixed. What is most fascinating about the psychotic is that very few were born that way. They were normally functioning people who became psychotic at some point in their lives. Understanding what prompted this transition from normalcy into psychoses, perhaps with a stop along the way in neurosis, would be of tremendous value in both intervening to stop the transition as well as reversing it once it has happened. What stresses and strains prompt the brain to create the delusional thoughts of the psychotic? Could they be related to the biobehavioral imperatives?

We have seen how failure to achieve the goals of the biobehavioral imperatives can create depression. Most of us, however, have ways of coping. We may fail at being "king of the hill" in the office, but we find other ways to make ourselves feel proud. For example, we can try woodworking or, if that does not work out, we can turn to gardening. Somehow we find something to achieve that allows us to feel good about ourselves.

Another method our mind uses to help us deal with frustration is called "selective thinking." When our boss gives us a performance review, in our own minds we may accentuate the positive and eliminate the negative. We may engage in a little distortion to makes things a bit less threatening. When our child begins to show behavior that is troubling, we may create thoughts to minimize its importance. In the normal course of our daily lives we often times engage in these little thought distortions, known in psychotherapy as denial and repression, that make us feel better about how things are going.

However, in some cases, we may meet with catastrophic failure to achieve the goals of one or even multiple biobehavioral imperatives. The mini-distortions of reality cannot make up for the grossly evident failure. For a lack of any one of a variety of talents, abilities, or coping skills, our brain senses that we have failed completely and have no alternatives to fulfill the very intense drive to accomplish these imperatives. What happens then?

Under the intense pressure to have a territory, be top dog, and be sexual, the brain increases the level of distortion of selective thinking, denial, and repression to the point that it creates a significant break with reality. The brain creates a delusional system so our mind feels that it has achieved its goals.

When a bag lady wheels her grocery cart full of possessions, is this her psychotic distortion of reality that allows her to successfully achieve nesting behaviors? Is a mentally ill person living in a cardboard box actually creating a territory to call his own and one that he can successively defend? *The delusional thoughts and reasons that form the mental system of the psychotic are the brain's attempt to create a reality that allows it to sense that the biobehavioral imperatives have been successfully accomplished.*

PSYCHOTHERAPY

One of the goals of any attempt to understand the biological systems of our body is of course to be able to fix that system when it breaks. Virtually all treatments for our body's ills have come about from the understanding of how the biology of our body operates. If the theory of the biobehavioral imperatives and how they control our thoughts and reasons is valid, then that theory should produce a way of treating the abnormal thoughts and reasons of mental illness.

The current treatment of mental illness utilizes one or sometimes both of two techniques. One is to use drugs that are known to alter the chemistry of the brain and to produce changes in our thoughts, emotions, and behaviors. Proof enough of the biological nature of the human mind. The other technique is through a therapist talking with patients and applying the theories of psychotherapy to help them understand their behavior. From this understanding and the potential it provides for the patients to modify their behavior, it is hoped that the patients will be able to achieve a happier life.

In the late nineteenth century, Sigmund Freud began development of his comprehensive theory of the mind. From this theory he then proposed a method of treatment for the disorders of neuroses and psychoses that afflicted psychiatric patients. Freud's theory was very complex and had many parts to it; however, the core of his theory was sexuality. For Freud, the entirety of mankind's productive efforts was a result of the sublimation of the forces of our sex drive.

Numerous other scientists of the mind were attracted to Freud and his ideas and came to Vienna to become a part of the group that developed these new theories of the mind. Two of the most important members of Freud's group were Carl Jung and Alfred Adler. They both were initial advocates of Freud and worked with Freud to expand on his theories of the mind and to develop a productive treatment method of psychotherapy that they called psychoanalysis.

Both Adler and Jung, however, came to disagree with Freud and set out to develop their own theories of the mind and methods of psychotherapy based upon their modification of Freud's initial theories. As did Freud, both Adler and Jung sought the root causes of human behavior. They disagreed with Freud over the crucial and central role of human sexuality.

Carl Jung developed a theory of the mind that centered on a concept called the "collective unconscious," a group of motivations that humankind has inherited from its animal ancestors. Jung spent a great deal of time traveling the world, visiting with primitive peoples in search of these instinctual drives in their purest form. In developing his theories, Jung used the term "archetypes." As described in his own words, "The archetypes are the unconscious images of the instincts themselves, in other words, that they are patterns of instinctual behavior." For Jung, Freud's focus on sexuality was too limiting. Jung wanted to expand the theory of the mind to include a larger array of instinctual drives that we have inherited from our animal ancestors and pass on genetically from one generation of human to the next.

Alfred Adler, in a similar vein, also thought Freud's single- minded focus on sexuality was too limiting. Adler developed a theory of the mind that gave great importance to man's striving to achieve goals and power. From Adler's perspective, man's behavior was an attempt to raise himself from a position of "inferiority" to one of "superiority." Adler's method of psychotherapy focused upon an analysis by the therapist and patient of the patient's need to achieve goals and thereby raise the standing of his or her position in the world. The concept of the "inferiority complex" came from Alfred Adler.

The three dominant figures in the development of psychoanalysis were Freud, Jung, and Adler. From their theories came our modern methods of psychotherapy. If these three pioneers of the mind had known what we know today about animal behavior, I wonder how their theories would have turned out. If they had access to the material on wolves, chimps, gorillas, and other animals that so clearly shows the importance of not just sexuality, but territoriality, and dominance hierarchies, perhaps their theories would not be very different from the ideas in *The Animal within Us*. In Carl Jung's work, it is striking how his use of the collective unconscious and the archetypes ring true to the genetically inherited behavior patterns we call the biobehavioral imperatives. Similarly, Alfred Adler and his theories of goals, power, and superiority sound so much like the need to achieve a top ranking in a dominance hierarchy. Of course, another biobehavioral imperative, sexuality, was at the heart of Freud's thinking.

GROWING UP RIGHT

A key component to Freud and his followers' theories of the mind was the importance of early development. For humans, that the events of childhood play a critical role in shaping the personality of the adult should not be surprising. As shown in the following description by Jane Goodall from *Through a Window* it is true for our animal ancestors.

Patrolling the boundaries is but one of the many duties that the young male chimpanzee must learn if he is to grow up to be a useful member of society. His adult experiences will be very different from those of a female. Thus it is not surprising that the milestones along the path he follows towards social maturity are different from those that mark the route for the female. Some, of course, are shared—such as the weaning process and the birth of a new baby in the family. But the initial break with the mother and the first journeys with the adult males not only come much earlier for the young male than for the female, but are of far greater significance. For it is here that he must learn many of the skills that he will need as an adult. The young male must challenge the females of his community, one by one, and then, when all have been dominated, he must begin to work his way into the dominance hierarchy of the adult males. The way in which the young male tackles each of these tasks, and the age at which he passes from one milestone to the next, depend heavily on his early family environment and the nature of his social experiences....

When Prof was two years old, for example, he was attacked by an adult male colobus monkey during a hunt. Passion was just sitting and watching, holding Prof, when suddenly one of the colobus males, enraged, leapt at and attacked her. She was quite unharmed: Prof had one toe bitten right off.

That experience, both painful and frightening, apparently left Prof with a deep-rooted fear of monkeys. Most young males begin to hunt when they are mere juveniles. Freud caught his first monkey (which Fifi took from him) when he was only six years old. Prof was not observed to hunt monkeys at all until he was eleven, and even at that it was in a half-hearted manner.

Growing up right is an issue that plagues parents. Members of each generation look back and focus on the ways their own childhoods went awry and swear they will not make the same mistakes with their own children. Yet generation after generation, parents continue to visit the psychiatrists' couches to try to understand where they went wrong and how to make it right.

From the perspective of the biobehavioral imperatives, it is clear that our biological brain goes through certain reliable patterns as the infant progresses toward adulthood. Studies by the animal behaviorists prove that much of what the brain is engaged in as a child is practice for the responsibilities of an adult. The responsibilities of an adult are to successfully engage in those behaviors that provide for the species survival, the biobehavioral imperatives.

Most important for parents obsessed with getting it right are the implications of the need for the animal going through puberty to begin its differentiation from the parent and finding a territory to call its own. Recall in Lesson IX the rebellious teenage baboon, Sherlock. No matter how "perfect" a parent may be, the interaction of changing hormones and brain circuits forces the child to leave the nest. The *echo speech* of the teenager's mind provides a *reasoned* thought pattern for that rebellious behavior. *No matter the actual facts of their childhood, they must come up with reasons to explain their biologically driven behavior of leaving the nest. It may be only natural that during a certain time in a person's life they will resent their parents.*

BIOBEHAVIORAL THERAPY

One of the main themes of the therapeutic approach of psychotherapy is for the patient to come to understand the unconscious motivations for their actions. A great deal of time in therapy is spent trying to find the unconscious motivations for why we engage in our behaviors. Once the patient uncovers the unconscious motives for their behavior, this understanding allows them to alter their behavior for the better. If Freud, Adler, and Jung had access to today's knowledge of evolution, genes, chromosomes, and animal behavior would they have used the biobehavioral imperatives as the actual unconscious motivations behind our actions?

A new psychotherapy could be built around the biobehavioral imperatives of territory, sexuality, and dominance as our unconscious motivations. It would be fascinating to apply the same techniques that Freud and his followers developed but instead utilize the biobehavioral imperatives as the framework for the interchange between therapist and patient. Therapy sessions would consist of the therapist leading the patient through a psychoanalysis of their thoughts and feelings in the context of their attempts to achieve the goals of their biobehavioral imperatives.

With an understanding of the true motivations behind our behavior, we should be able to either change to more productive behaviors, or just from gaining insight into our motivations, come to a greater inner peace about why we do what we do.

For example, if we are feeling depressed, we should examine our jobs, our family life, our relationships with our friends and see if we are engaged in dominance struggles. We should examine our actions as if we were an animal in a pride, competing for a position of dominance.

If failures at work are the source of our depression, biobehavioral therapy would help the patient understand their depression in terms of their failure to achieve a sense of dominance in their work place. Once we understand our behavior in those terms, we can accurately assess our chances of achieving our work-place goals. If it turns out we probably cannot win a promotion, it would make sense to change jobs.

As previously discussed, the mid-life career crisis is just such an event: feelings of anxiety and depression that are the emotional counterpart of a frustration in achieving dominance in our career. For those who see that they probably will never be king of the hill, finding another hill by changing their career may be the only reasonable solution.

Biobehavioral therapy would focus on helping a patient to achieve a sense of self-esteem, the emotional counterpart to dominance achieved. Self-esteem is well known as the key to alleviating many neurotic symptoms such as depression.

Sadly, it is unreasonable to expect that we will meet with nothing but success in everything that we do. Failure to achieve success, with its attendant loss of self-esteem, is only to be expected in the complex lives we lead. How, then, can we manage to keep our chins up and maintain a relatively steady sense of self-esteem and self-worth?

Fortunately, our nimble human brain can create any one of a number of activities that will allow us to do better within another hierarchy. Our human mind's creation of noncareer activities such as hobbies attests to our inventiveness in creating new arenas in which we can play-out our need for dominance. Hobbies, such as the best collection of model trains or developing high-level wood working skills, are activities in which we can become an expert. The moral superiority of volunteer work on behalf of those less privileged than ourselves is by itself an act of dominance, regardless of how well we do at the activity. Our human lives are filled with alternative behaviors that give us more than one arena in which to achieve the goals of our biobe-havioral imperatives.

The history of the development of psychotherapies shows that it is possible through a verbal exchange between a therapist and patient for the patient to come to a better understanding of themselves. This understanding at times allows the patient to feel better about them-selves and to change their behavior in a positive fashion. Under-standing behavior from the perspective of the biobehavioral impera-tives should provide a clear and concise psychoanalysis that will allow the patient to alter their behavior in ways that allows them to become more productive in achieving the goals of the biobehavioral impera-tives and to experience the attendant feelings of enhanced self-esteem.

LESSON XIII
The Criminal Animal

As would be predicted from the concept of genetics and statistical averages most peoples behavioral programs are similar. Therefore without much trouble we all obey the laws, get up every day, and try to achieve the shared goals of the biobehavioral imperatives. However, the *ying* of the concept of statistical average has its *yang*—biological variability. Some people do not have the same programs. For them, it is very difficult to live within the order and structure of society, and when they break its laws, we call them criminals. Tremendous insight can be gained into the criminal mind by analyzing its motivations, reasons, and lack of socialized control from the perspective of the animal within us.

For most of us the neural circuitry that holds the programs for the imperatives is quite similar, reflecting the clustering of biological variability around average values. Our societies' laws and standards of conduct, both written and unwritten, reflect those thoughts and behaviors in which most of us engage *naturally*.

We quite easily live our lives according to the rules and regulations set for us by our conscious minds under the control of our humankind's imperatives. It is no accident that for most of us living a psychologically content and law abiding life is not difficult since the same imperatives controlling our behavior are at the origins of the thoughts that created the laws governing our behavior. With our active frontal lobes, we inhibit the reflex animal response and substitute a response we have been taught by an ordered and civilized society.

The existence of law and order is a testimony to the regulatory functions of the frontal lobe that allow us to channel the biobehavioral imperatives into derivative behaviors that make for a complex and lawful society.

However, for some, the normalcy and contentment of thoughts and behavior that is shared by most is a sometime thing. For these people, their thoughts and behaviors do not provide them with a life of mainstream behaviors or psychological tranquility. The aberrant thoughts and behaviors of the criminal represent a deviation from the normal operation of the neural circuitry.

If the criminal mind fails to fulfill a biobehavioral imperative, the animal is unleashed, and it may even kill to achieve its goal.

THE ANIMAL UNLEASHED

In the case of a criminal, the frontal lobe is unable to regulate the actions of the biobehavioral imperatives. If a thief wants an object, he takes it, outside the rules of acquisition normally followed by a member of a society. If a murderer feels threatened, he kills the challenger, outside the rules society has established to deal with such challenges. The frontal lobe is unable to inhibit these responses so that the person can then channel their motivations into socially acceptable behaviors. The drive of the biobehavioral imperatives provides the thoughts and reasons in a criminal's mind that lead to and justify these behaviors.

The case of rape is a particularly heinous form of fulfilling our sexual and dominance needs. In his book, *The Hot House*, which examines several cases of criminals in a maximum security prison, Pete Early describes a convicted murderer discussing his rape of a fellow inmate:

> It really didn't have nothing to do with sex. It had to do with power. All my life, people been fucking me, and when I was fucking that kid, I hated what I was doing, but I loved it too, because it was me on top and there wasn't one fucking thing he could do to stop me. Nothing. I was in charge, complete control.
>
> I could have done whatever the fuck I wanted to him and it is a fucking amazing feeling when you feel that way.

The same inmate discussed a heterosexual liaison: "A young filly doesn't chase after a weak or crippled horse. She picks the strongest stallion in the pack and runs after him."

Criminals are people for whom the biobehavioral imperatives are at the tips of their tongues, on the uppermost surface of their conscious lives. The frontal lobe seems to have lost its effectiveness in inhibiting and regulating the immediate behavioral responses of the imperatives. Criminals cannot channel the energy, motivation, and drive of the biobehavioral imperatives into learned and socially acceptable behaviors. *Of course since criminals' thoughts and reasons are controlled by the same imperatives that control their behaviors, the biobehavioral imperatives also provide the intellectual justification that precedes the criminal act.*

The assassination of public figures shows perfectly how murder is driven by uninhibited biobehavioral imperatives, in this case dominance. It would seem that the assassination of political leaders should always come from the rationale of political meaning. The assassination of President Kennedy by Lee Harvey Oswald is one in which it appears that political feelings were of little importance. Oswald's history of political activism at first suggested a political motive, yet comments by acquaintances and family showed that he was a failed little man looking for a way to be somebody. The attempted assassination of President Reagan by John Hinkley seems to have been a pure case of murderous actions taken by a person who was desperate for dominance. In terms of wanting to kill a political figure, the President of the United States, Hinkley had no political motivations whatsoever. Interestingly, he also had set his sights on an actress, Jodie Foster, another potential victim, whose murder would bring him the dominance and notoriety he had yet to achieve.

BAD STARTS

The experiences of our early years are important in understanding the psychology not only of the neurotic and psychotic adult, but of the criminal as well. The relationship between early experience and criminality is dramatically demonstrated in the following account of the relationship between a baby chimp and its mother. As we shall see from Jane van Lawick-Goodall's description in *In the Shadow of Man* what may be the only documented mother and daughter team of serial killers in the animal kingdom grew out of some highly abnormal early experiences.

It was, however, very different for Pom, one of the first female infants born into our group. Her mother, Passion, actually laid the baby on the ground the very first day of her life and allowed two young females to touch and even groom her as she lay there. But then, in all respects, Passion was a somewhat unnatural mother.

If her treatment of Pom was anything to go by, I suspect Passion had lost other infants, too, for Pom had to fight for her survival right from the start.

But Passion usually ignored Pom's whimpers completely; if she couldn't find the nipple by herself it was just bad luck. If Pom happened to be suckling when Passion wanted to move off, she seldom waited until the infant had finished her meal; she just got up and went, and Pom, clinging for once under her mother, struggled to keep the nipple in her mouth as long as she could before she was relentlessly pushed up onto Passion's back. As a result of her mother's lack of solicitude, Pom seldom managed to suckle for more than two minutes at a time before she was interrupted by Passion, and often it was much less. Most infants during their first years suckle for about three minutes once an hour. Pom probably made up for her shorter feeds by suckling more frequently.

Passion was positively callous. One day, previous to which Pom had never been seen to totter on her own for more than two yards, Passion suddenly got up and walked away from her infant. Pom, struggling to follow and falling continually, whimpered louder each time, and finally her mother returned and shoved the infant onto her back. This happened repeatedly. As Pom learned to walk better, Passion did not even bother to return when the infant cried—she just waited for her to catch up by herself.

Dr. Goodall describes the horrific consequences of this aberrant upbringing in *Through a Window*.

When Derek and I got to Gombe we heard the horrific story in gruesome detail. Gilka, we were told, was sitting peacefully in the afternoon sun, cradling her tiny infant, when Passion suddenly appeared. She stood for a moment, looking at mother and child—then charged towards them, hair bristling. Gilka fled, screaming, but she was doubly handicapped—with an infant to support and a crippled wrist. In a flash she was overtaken. Passion leapt upon her and seized hold of little Otta. Gilka tried desperately to save her baby, but she had no chance and after the briefest of struggles Passion succeeded in snatching Otta away. Then, most macabre of all, she pressed the stolen baby to her breast, and Otta clung there desperately while Passion again leapt on Gilka. At this moment Pom, an adolescent at the time, rushed to join her mother, and Gilka, outnumbered, turned and fled with Passion in hot pursuit, Otta still clinging tightly to her belly. Confident in her victory, Passion sat on the ground, pulled the terrified infant from her breast, and bit deeply into the front of the little head: death was instantaneous. Slowly, with utmost caution, Gilka returned. When she was close enough to see the limp and bleeding corpse she gave a single loud, bark-like sound—of horror? despair?—and then turned and left.

For the next five hours Passion fed on Gilka's baby, sharing the flesh with her family, Pom and juvenile Prof. Between them they consumed it all, every last scrap.

The following year Gilka gave birth to a healthy son....

It was inevitable that, sooner or later, Passion would encounter Gilka when there were no males nearby to help. It happened when Gilka, in the heat of midday, was resting with her infant in the shade. Orion was three weeks old. Pom arrived first, moving silently from the undergrowth. She stood watching mother and child for a moment, then lay down nearby....Five minutes later Passion appeared. Pom at once hurried towards her mother and reached to touch her back, a wide grin of excitement on her face. It was the sort of interaction that occurs between mother and daughter when they get close to a tree laden with delicious fruit. As one, Passion and Pom charged Gilka who, at first sight of Passion, had begun to flee. Gilka screamed and screamed as she ran, but there were no males nearby to respond to her desperate appeal for help.

Pom raced ahead of Gilka who veered to the side, trying to avoid her. At that moment Passion caught up, seized hold of Gilka and threw her to the ground. Gilka did not try to fight, but crouched protectively over her precious baby. Pom then flung herself into the fray, hitting and stamping on Gilka while Passion seized hold of the infant and bit at its head. Gilka vainly hit at her murderous attacker, while with her free hand she clung desperately to Orion. Passion bit Gilka's face and blood poured down from deep laceration on her brow. Then, working as a team, Passion and Pom together turned Gilka onto her back and while the stronger Passion grappled with the mother, Pom seized the baby and ran off with him. Then she sat and bit deep into the front of his head. And so Orion was killed in the same brutal ways as little Otta the year before.

Gilka wrenched herself free from Passion and raced after Pom but Passion was onto her in a flash, attacking her yet again, biting her hands and feet. Gilka, bleeding now from countless wounds, made a last valiant attempt to retrieve her mutilated infant, but it was hopeless. And then Passion, leaving Gilka, took the prey and hurried off, followed by Pom. Young Prof, who had watched the life and death struggle from the safety of a tree, climbed down and ran after his mother. Gilka limped after them for a short way but she was soon left far behind and after a few minutes she gave up and began to lick and dab at her wounds. The Passion family, meanwhile, vanished silently into the forest.

Suddenly a twig snapped: I turned sharply and found, to my horror, that Passion and Pom had approached, moving almost without sound on the soft, wet, forest floor. Now they stood, motionless, staring up towards Melissa and her babies. None of the chimps above had seen them. With slow, stealthy movements Pom started to climb towards Melissa. Passion, heavily pregnant, climbed as well, but she soon stopped and watched from a low branch. Pom, creeping very quietly, got closer and closer and I was just about to yell a warning when suddenly Melissa saw them. Instantly she began to scream, loudly and urgently and, reckless in her panic, took a huge leap through space, towards the nearest branch of the next tree, the babies supported only by her thighs. My heart was thudding but somehow all three made it and Melissa hurried to sit close to Satan—who had stopped feeding and was watching Pom intently. Melissa, with one hand laid on the big male's shoulders, turned and barked her defiance at the younger female. And so the attempt was foiled.

KEEPING THE LEASH ON

The criminal act is the biobehavioral imperative, the animal within us, let out of its cage of the law and order of social constraints. The inhibitory frontal lobe is no longer functioning to regulate our behavior and channel the behaviors driven by the imperatives into the appropriate forms of socially acceptable behavior. Key to this story is the appreciation that the thoughts and reasons that lead us to act the way we do are themselves produced by the biobehavioral imperatives. It is hoped that the concept of the biobehavioral imperatives and the relationship between these imperatives and our thoughts, reasons, and behavior may provide valuable insight into our understanding of the criminal mind and provide us with ways of allowing this mind to fulfill the goals of its imperatives in a less destructive manner.

LESSON XIV
The Passionate Animal

The ideas in *The Animal within Us* present a strong case that our human mind with its thoughts, reasons, and conscious self-awareness has its origins in the biobehavioral programs wired into the neural circuits of our brain. These programs make us act, think, and say the things that we do. These same programs are a part of our inheritance from our animal ancestors. This perspective is an awfully mechanical and cold view of our humanity. The same humanity of love, hate, poetry, flights of fancy and a soul. Is there a place for human emotions, the passions that we feel, in such a view of the human mind? Or perhaps the answer is that animals experience emotional feelings in much the same way that we humans do? If we all share the same molecules and brain cells, why not?

The Animal within Us presents a fact-based, analytical, and logical approach to understanding the origins of our human mind in our animal-like and biological brain. So far there has been very little emotional warmth or feeling displayed or discussed. Our human behaviors, from our belief and prayer to God and our sports and business activities to a mother's bond with her child, have all been presented as if they were performed by computer-controlled mechanical beings—programs in our brain, circuits of neurons, stimulus followed by response—without *passion nor feelings*.

Is there room for human emotion in such an approach? No question we humans do feel pain and pleasure and sorrow and joy. In fact, minute by minute, every day of our lives, we have a continual and ever-present sense of emotional experience. If the ideas in *The Animal within Us* are correct, then no aspect of our humanity can be left out. Can the neural circuits of the biobehavioral imperatives in our animal-like brain experience emotions? Or are we alone in the animal kingdom in our ability to experience passions?

The clenched fist, tense muscles, and facial grimace of rage, the down-turned mouth and stooped shoulders of sadness, or the wide-eyed, big smile and open-armed, joyful greeting of an old friend are emotions expressed through muscle movements. Specific sounds are made in association with these feelings: the laughter of happiness or the mournful wail of sadness, sounds that are produced by muscle movements. Primitive tribes across the globe who have had no contact with the outside world all possess very similar patterns of emotional expressions. Evidently, then, just as we all have a five-fingered hand, these patterns of muscle movements, also known as our emotional expressions, come precoded in our human genes.

Emotional expressions are in fact patterns of muscle movements programmed in our genes. We have been taught to apply certain word labels such as "angry," "sad," or "happy" to these specific and easily differentiable patterns of muscle movements common to all human beings. That is why we can recognize anger, sadness, and happiness in people no matter where they are from. These emotions are a universally shared part of the human genetic make-up.

Surely there must be more to human emotions than just word labels attached to patterns of muscle movements encoded in our genes and neural circuits. How about our internal sensations of these emotions, the pain of sorrow or the ebullience of joy? Sure, we can tell when other people have feelings of anger or joy by observing their behavior and listening to the qualities of the sounds they make, but we also *feel* these emotions. We *feel* angry and we *feel* sad. These *feelings* are essential to that which makes us human.

In the same way that our eyes and ears are sensors for the lights and sounds of the outside world, inside our body we have sensors for the inside world, what the legendary nineteenth-century biologist Claude Bernard labeled as the "internal milieu." Thanks to sensors for the internal milieu we feel hungry when our stomachs are empty and full after we have eaten. When we feel angry, not only do the exterior parts of our body that can be observed by others undergo changes, but our interior parts change as well. Our heart rate changes, our blood pressure changes, the secretions of our stomach change, and other of our internal organs undergo specific changes associated with each of our emotions. These changes in the internal milieu provoke sensations, or *feelings* within the sensory systems of our internal milieu. We humans, and perhaps animals as well, *sense* our emotional *feelings* in the same way we *feel* the sense of sight and sound.

Just as an outside observer sees our behavior and then puts the learned word of "anger" to what he observes, the same occurs inside our brain in the case of the sensations of our internal milieu. As a result of the learning process that we underwent in our childhood, we will apply the appropriate word label of either anger, joy, or sadness, to the sensations from the internal milieu that are being felt by our brain.

That some feelings are painful and unpleasant and we try to avoid them while others are enjoyable and we try to make them happen is not an accident but a result of evolutionary selection. The sensations from a bodily injury (a threat to our survival) we experience as painful and the sensations from sugar (a necessary energy source) are pleasurable. If it were not this way, then why would we avoid injury to our body and pursue necessary nutrients? Creatures that did not experience bodily injury as pain and eating sweets as pleasurable became extinct.

The same principles hold true for the biobehavioral imperatives. Achieving the goals of the imperatives is necessary for survival and therefore are experienced as pleasurable. There is no greater pleasure for a woman than raising her child. Similarly, failure to achieve an imperative is painful. There is no greater sadness than the death of a child. The law of the survival of the fittest has seen to it that we maximize joy and minimize sadness by pursuing or avoiding events that evoke these "emotional" experiences and thereby perpetuate our species.

ANIMAL FEELINGS

If our emotional expressions and feelings have their origins in our animal-like brain's biology, then we must ask the next logical question. Do animals have the same feelings and sense of emotional experiences? The following excerpts are from books written by experts in the objective analysis of animal behavior. These are not the warm-hearted dog lovers who treat their pets as one of their own children and who chatter on in an anthropomorphic fashion over "Fifi's" feelings. Yet they are human beings who learned as children to place certain labels such as "fear," "joy," and "anger" upon certain patterns of behavior that they observed in other people and that they felt themselves through their internal milieu. Let us see how these cold hearted and objective scientists reacted to the patterns of muscle movements that they observed in the wild. Jane Goodall describes her own and the responses of others who study chimps in *Through a Window*.

In fact, all those who have worked long and closely with chimpanzees have no hesitation in asserting that chimps experience emotions similar to those which in ourselves we label pleasure, joy, sorrow, anger, boredom and so on. Some of the emotional states of the chimpanzee are so obviously similar to ours that even an inexperienced observer can understand what is going on. An infant who hurls himself screaming to the ground, face contorted, hitting out with his arms at any nearby object, banging his head, is clearly having a tantrum. Another youngster, who gambols around his mother, turning somersaults, pirouetting and, every so often, rushing up to her and tumbling into her lap, patting her or pulling her hand towards him in a request for tickling, is obviously filled with *joie de vivre*. There are few observers who would not unhesitatingly ascribe his behaviour to a happy, carefree state of wellbeing. And one cannot watch chimpanzee infants for long without realizing that they have the same emotional need for affection and reassurance as human children. An adult male, reclining in the shade after a good meal, reaching benignly to play with an infant or idly groom an adult female, is clearly in a good mood. When he sits with bristling hair, glaring at his subordinates and threatening them, with irritated gestures, if they come too close, he is clearly feeling cross and grumpy. We make these judgements because the similarity of so much of a chimpanzee's behaviour to our own permits us to empathize.

Who has not witnessed the joy and glee of a victory celebration by human beings that is not a perfect match for the following joyous romp described by Dr. Goodall in *In the Shadow of Man*?

Goliath and William arrived together on Christmas morning and gave loud screams of excitement when they saw the huge pile of fruit. They flung their arms around one another and Goliath kept patting William on his wide-open screaming mouth while William laid one arm over Goliath's back.

...as the group of chimps which had been following him suddenly saw the bananas all over the path. With piercing shrieks of excitement they hugged and kissed and patted one another as they fell on the unexpected feast.

The look in someone's eyes is perhaps the most important cue we humans use when we try to understand what is going on in other people's minds, in particular what emotions they are feeling. Whether it is the importance of "eye contact" during a job interview or the staring down of an opponent made famous during the dominance battle between Sonny Liston and Muhammad Ali for the heavyweight championship of the world, the look in someone's eye has a long tradition in our human culture. Liston and Ali could have taken a lesson from the gorillas described by George Schaller in *The Year of the Gorilla.*

These giants of the forest, each with the strength of several men, were settling their differences, whatever they were, not by fighting but rather by trying to stare each other down. They stared at each other threateningly for from twenty to thirty seconds, but neither gave in, and they parted.

For all of us who spend time watching wildlife through binoculars, the following thoughts by Shirley Strum in *A Journey into the World of Baboons* may give us pause the next time we want a close view of a grizzly.

I was always careful at whom I looked; when I came face to face with one of the animals, I'd lower my eyes or turn away my head. It was for this reason that I was unable to wear sunglasses, despite the wind and the blinding light; the first animals to catch a glimpse of me wearing them ran off in obvious terror. Small wonder: to them, the glasses not only covered my own eyes, obliterating important visual communication, but presented them with the biggest, wide-eye threat they'd ever seen.

It is interesting to speculate on how many *unprovoked* attacks by grizzlies may have had their origins in a hiker staring through the big, dark, and threatening eyes of binoculars.

One of the great hunters of Africa, Carl Akeley, was swayed to never hunt again by his empathetic moment of eye-to-eye contact after killing the mother of a gorilla child. The scene is described by Penelope Bodry-Sanders in *Carl Akeley, Africa's Collector, Africa's Savior.*

> Here he stood, locked in a moment of profound contact with a living gorilla, and what he saw in the youngster's eyes were emotions of terror and pain—familiar emotions registered in familiar ways. In that face he saw kinship, intelligence, and sensitivity.

Finally, our true relationship with our animal ancestors is so touchingly described by Walter Baumgartel in *Up among the Mountain Gorillas.*

> The little fellow looked first at Reuben, then at me, and was obviously puzzled by our strange appearance. We must have been the first humans he had ever seen. When he realized he was left alone with such uncanny company, his courage failed and the frightened creature turned and ran back into the forest. Mother, now missing her child, returned just in time to see his little bottom disappear. She chased him, grabbed him by the hand, gave him a slap on the backside, and dragged him over the path into the forest, where Father's impatient barking could be heard.
>
> This family scene, so touchingly human, changed my attitude toward gorillas. From that moment on, they were no longer mere animals to me; they were relatives and there was no reason to be ashamed of the kinship.

These quotations show quite clearly how we infer the mental states, the emotions of others, from the pattern of muscle movements that we observe. That emotional states of the animals are inferred as being similar to emotional states of humans should not be surprising since the muscle movement programs are similar in both human and animal brains. When activated, these programs produce near-identical patterns of integrated muscle movements, behaviors from which we infer the emotional state. These examples of animal-human interactions also demonstrate not only the similarity between the muscle movement programs contained in the brains of humans and animals, but also, and equally as important, the similarities in which we respond to these behavioral displays, whether they come from our closest life-long friend or a chimpanzee or gorilla in the jungle.

The Animal Brain And The Human Mind

The Animal within Us has shown the origins of our human behavior in patterns of behavior we have inherited from our animal ancestors, the biobehavioral imperatives. These imperatives are the source of the way we structure our societies and their social institutions. In addition, they drive the very thoughts, feelings, and reasons that we create to explain why we behave the way that we do. From war and peace between nations to love and hate between people, the biobehavioral imperatives are in control. If we come to understand the origins of our thoughts and feelings in these terms, it is possible to come to grips with the forces that drive our behavior. If we each learn to tame the beast within us, it is possible that we can make our own personal animals lead a life that has us wagging our tails in pleasure and psychological contentment as often as possible.

The people of the sixteenth and seventeenth centuries were shocked by the revolutionary theories of Copernicus and Galileo. Their ideas suggested that natural forces, not God, created and controlled the universe. The earth and humankind were not the center of the universe but just one of a great many planets. Charles Darwin then added an additional affront to God and the human ego. According to Darwin, not only were we humans not the true children of God, but we were the great-great-great...great-grandchildren of some form of monkey.

The past century has seen nothing but confirmation of the ideas of Copernicus, Galileo, and Darwin. Astronomy placed the earth as just another planet among millions of other planets. Neuroscience has shown that our human brain is far more similar to an animal brain than it is different. The animal behaviorists have shown just how similar are patterns of human and animal behavior. Yet we humans do think, we also reason, we have emotions, and we are conscious of our thinking, reasoning, and our emotional feelings. We have religion, with its God and its prayers. We still feel we are special, not just some highly evolved form of animal.

The ideas in *The Animal within Us* add to the revolution begun by Copernicus, Galileo, and Darwin by showing that these uniquely human qualities of our mind can also be understood as a product of our biological and animal-like human brain. Even religion, with its God and prayer, is itself a product of the forces of nature, thoughts, and behaviors forced upon us by the behavioral programs inherited from our animal ancestors, the biobehavioral imperatives.

The Animal within Us proposed in its "Introduction" to resolve the paradox of our human mind in our animal brain by developing a transfer equation. The example given of a transfer equation was the formula $F = 9/5C + 32$, which transfers a temperature from degrees Centigrade (C) into the equivalent degrees Fahrenheit (F). The goal of this book is to develop a transfer equation that allows the ideas and concepts of the brain and its biology to be transferred into the ideas and concepts of the mind and its psyche. If this could be achieved, the results would be of tremendous value in understanding not only our own behavior as individuals but also our behavior in social groups.

The main girders for the bridge between the brain and the mind are the biobehavioral imperatives of territoriality, dominance hierarchies, and sexuality. We have seen how the biobehavioral imperatives are the origin of our mind. They create the thoughts and reasons of not only the normally functioning mind but of the aberrant—criminal or mentally ill—mind as well. Religions with their gods and prayers are a creation of our mind in order to fulfill a need to be a member of a pack with a dominant leader who sees to our safety. The enterprise of business and the pursuit of money, the preoccupation of most of our waking hours, is a complex system devised by our mind so that we can still spend our days acting out our biobehavioral imperatives. Our human wars to the death as well as their resolution short of total annihilation are based upon behavior programs millions of years old that provide for the marking and defense of territories and the possessions within them. The games we play, the teams and stars for whom we cheer, and the great joy sports brings to us, all are a part of the neuronal circuitry we share with our animal ancestors.

THE MIND-BRAIN TRANSFER EQUATION

It is now time to integrate all these ideas into the transfer equation between the biological brain we have inherited from our animal ancestors and the human mind. The components of the transfer equation as shown in Figure 3 are:

First, the biobehavioral imperatives (*BBI*) for territoriality (*t*), dominance (*d*), and sexuality (*s*): *BBI(t,d,s)*

Second, the stimuli (*S*) that prompt us to behave. These stimuli come from the external world (*e*), such as a trespasser into our territory or from our body's internal world (*i*), such as a feeling of hunger: *S(e,i)*

Third, our own personal history of the outcomes of our behavior, memory (*m*). What behaviors did we try and what were the results? How successful were we when we tried one behavior and how successful were we when we tried another behavior? This is the outcome history (*OH*) of our behaviors: *OH(m)*

Fourth, human reason (*R*). The pattern of thoughts structured by the biobehavioral imperatives that leads us to act the way that we do and that we use to justify a certain behavior: *R*

Fifth, our thoughts, our conscious self-awareness in the form of the silent *echo speech* (*ES*) that associative conditioning has developed within our brains: *ES*

Sixth, the actual behavior that we perform, the movement of our muscles that is our BEHAVIOR.

Seventh, the emotional experience we feel that accompanies the behavior:*E* Combining all these elements into one formula, we develop the following transfer equation.

As a practical matter, this is how it all works: During the course of our daily lives, the biobehavioral imperatives [*BBI(t,d,s)*] lie in a state between activation or quiescence. Which of the imperatives is controlling our behavior is a function of their relative level of activation. The activation level of each imperative is controlled by the stimuli [*S(e,i)*] that reach the brain from the external or internal world.

For example, we see an intruder into our territory, a guy walking down the street comes up our driveway. The visual stimulus [*S(e,i)*] of his presence activates the territorial imperative [*BBI(t)*]. Once an imperative is activated, BEHAVIOR is imminent. Our animal heritage wants us to give a roar, throw stones, or shoot the s.o.b. However, thanks to the regulatory control of our frontal lobe, we stop and give the matter some thought.

The specific response we give is chosen for us by our past outcome history [*OH(m)*] in dealing with intruders, the previous success or failure for a specific behavior in achieving the desired result. After thinking it through, do we get a gun and take a shot at the intruder, throw stones at him, or just ask him politely to leave?

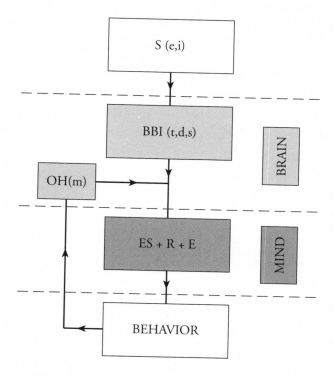

Fig. 3. The transfer equation which bridges the biology of the brain to the psychology of the mind, showing the process whereby activity in the brain creates the thoughts and feelings of the human mind which culminate in a behavioral act.

In this case, let us say we can tell it is a door-to-door salesman. That particular set of stimuli for a salesman is matched in our memory banks and we recall that a polite "No thank you, I don't want any" has in the past caused the intruder to retreat.

Of course, in our mind is a thought [*ES*] and a reason [*R*] as to how we should act. We do not say out loud to the person: "You are an intruder into my territory, I perceive you as a threat I can tell you are a salesman, and I do not want to talk to you. The last time someone like you came up my driveway, I asked him to leave and that got rid of him." Our frontal lobe inhibits us from saying that. We have been taught it would be impolite. Instead the associative conditioning process allows us to hear the *echo speech* [*ES*] of that thought as the reasons [R] behind our BEHAVIOR. All we actually say is, "No thank you, have a nice day."

The results of our response to the intruder are twofold. One is that the outcome of the behavior adds another piece of information to our memory storage. Second, the outcome of the behavior creates a new set of stimuli reaching our brain that either turns up or turns down the activation level of the imperative that prompted our behavior. In this case, if the salesman leaves, the activation level of the imperative for territory is turned down and no longer controls our behavior. If the salesman were to continue to walk up our driveway, the activation level would be increased and a more aggressive response given.

Accompanying our outward response to the intruder of taking a few steps toward him and speaking to him, is a response inside our body as well. Since an intruder is a threat, our blood pressure increases, our heart rate goes up, our pupils dilate and a variety of other such internal changes occur in our body. We experience this set of responses as unpleasant, negative reinforcers. That is why our body gives a response to get the intruder to go away. In addition, we have been taught to associate the word "fear" with these internal sensations. In this way, we experience the emotional (E) aspects of an intruder into our territory.

WE HAVE NOW BRIDGED THE GAP BETWEEN THE BIOLOGY OF OUR BRAIN AND THE PSYCHE AND FEEL-INGS OF OUR MIND.

YOUR OWN BEST BEAST

I sincerely hope that from the ideas presented within this book that the reader will be able to lead a life that will have the animal within them wagging its tail as often as possible.

A New Look At Old Questions

Viewing our human behavior through the perspective of our bio-genetic inheritance from our animal ancestors has taught us a great many things. We have learned why we believe and pray to a God, why we wage war and peace, why we spend most of our lives pursuing our career goals, and why we do and say all the other things that we do. Explaining our human thoughts, feelings, and reasons in this way also provides us with insights into some of the classical issues of philosophy. What additional lessons might our animal ancestors hold for us on some of the great dilemmas of philosophy?

The results of our inquiry into the biological nature of the human mind and the manner in which we have resolved the brain-mind duality raises several fascinating philosophical questions. First, if our reasons and our conscious decision making are controlled by the biobehavioral imperatives, where is our human freedom of choice, our free will? Second, are we human beings still evolving or have we reached an end point of the evolutionary road? Third, if our behavior is determined by behavioral programs that are so similar to those of our animal ancestors, what is our relationship to the animals? Are we humans really just like animals? Perhaps one could turn the question around and ask if animals are really just like humans? All of these questions are intriguing and important; each one of them is worthy of numerous books unto themselves. For our purpose we will simply frame these issues from the perspective of the ideas described in *The Animal within Us.*

FREE WILL

If our behaviors are determined by the imperatives that we inherit in our genes, how is it that humans can exercise free choice over their actions? If biology is truly destiny, what happens to the notion of our freedom to choose, our free will?

The *biological* imperatives, which make all humans have two eyes in the front of their heads and five fingers on each of their hands, and the *biobehavioral* imperatives are two different forms of the same biological process. Our human behaviors are just as preordained by our genes as is our growing a human hand. The biobehavioral imperatives say that in a given situation, the imperatives of territory, dominance, and sexuality will drive us to give a certain response. Not only that, but they will also control our reasoned thoughts, which at a conscious level provide the rationale behind our actions.

Free will, do we have it? Evidently not, if one accepts a strict interpretation of the biobehavioral imperatives and the control they exert over our lives and our thoughts. At the risk of sounding cavalier about the whole issue, may I suggest that the real question is not whether or not we truly have a free will but instead, do we think we have free will? René Descartes, the eminent seventeenth-century French philosopher, is remembered for his saying, "I think, therefore I am." Perhaps we must accept the saying, *"I think I have free will, therefore I do."*

END OF THE EVOLUTIONARY ROAD

Are the evolutionary forces of sexual and natural selection still at work shaping our human species? Or is humankind the final stopping point of evolution?

Humankind, with its fine control over its fingers, its binocular vision, its bipedal posture, and its sophisticated oral and written communication systems, has developed the ability to alter its environment. We can create artificial means, such as heating systems, irrigation, and the domestication of animals for food as a way of adapting to virtually any complex of environmental factors on the earth. The "natural" of natural selection is no longer at work. We can artificially adapt to any environment rather than letting genetic mutation and natural selection choose which version of us makes it to the next generation. We are now immune to the evolutionary forces of natural selection.

Similarly, it is no longer true that only the mightiest with the most robust genes mate with each other. In our animal ancestors this process of sexual selection saw to it that only those creatures with the most robust characteristics passed their genes on to the next generation. We humans have "equal opportunity" mating. The weaker and the weakest, the infirm, and the dolt can find a mate and insure the passing on of their genes to the next generation. Sexual selection has now joined natural selection as irrelevant. Perhaps we have reached an end to our traditional evolution.

Philosophers and political scientists have suggested that humankind's willingness to kill itself off in great numbers through a nuclear holocaust may be the only event that could alter the course of human evolution. If a nuclear doomsday were to occur, then those intellectual traits that made us human and allowed us to discover atomic power would have become their own force of natural selection and led us to our own extinction. However, even with our demise, life on earth would not end. Other, "lower" life forms would survive and the increased radiation would enhance the mutation of their genes and the processes of evolution would be off and running in an accelerated fashion.

ALL MOTHER NATURE'S CHILDREN

The last question for such philosophical musings is the relationship between humans and their animal ancestors. Scientifically, it is a fact that the molecules in our human body are identical to the molecules in an animal's body. The way these molecules are organized into organs such as the heart, lungs, and brain are amazingly similar between our nearest animal relatives and us humans. Human DNA and chimp DNA is remarkably similar. We share 99% of our DNA with our nearest animal ancestors. In fact, chimp DNA is more similar to human DNA than it is to gorilla DNA. These are hard, unambiguous, scientific facts.

However, we have always held the subjective opinion that somehow the intellectual processes of the human brain, its mind, were significantly different from the mind of an animal. Our human reason, thoughts, belief in God, emotions, and our conscious self-awareness are the main intellectual abilities that separate us from the animals.

The Animal within Us has explained that our human reason is the chain of thoughts that is driven by our biobehavioral imperatives so that we come to a conclusion that matches the behavior that our imperatives choose for us anyway. Our conscious self-awareness, the *echo speech* we sense, is a result of a neurobiological process called associative conditioning that occurs between the intention to speak and the sound that would have been made if we had spoken out loud. Recall the bear with paralyzed vocal chords. Did it hear itself go "woof" when the intruder entered into its territory? Does this sensing of the sound through the process of associative conditioning constitute self-awareness for the bear, and would the bear have thought his territorial defense as the only "reasonable" thing to do?

The emotions of anger, rage, fear, happiness, and joy were described as word labels we have given to patterns of muscle movements. When we see a person engaging in one of these movement patterns we apply the correct label to the pattern of muscle movements we observe and we infer they are "experiencing" a certain emotion. In excerpts from books about animal behavior we saw how behavioral scientists, upon observing certain patterns of muscle movements in chimpanzees and gorillas, could not help but infer human emotions from these expressions since they so mimicked our own.

Interesting questions to ponder: what goes on inside an animal's mind? Is it similar to what goes on inside our own mind? Do they experience the *echo speech* of thought, albeit limited in its complexity by the number of sounds they can make? Since they make some of the same patterns of muscle movements that we do, are they experiencing the same emotions? If one accepts the role of the biobehavioral imperatives in our human behaviors and accepts that our human imperatives are inherited from our animal ancestors and that their brains contain imperatives quite similar to ours, then one can certainly conclude that an animal's mind may not be as different from a human's mind as we once thought.

We explained our religions, Gods, and prayers by asserting that our biobehavioral imperative to be a part of a dominance hierarchy has driven our thoughts to create God and our act of submission to God, prayer. If we are correct, then God is a creation of our need to have a supreme being so that we humans may,

"walk through the valley of death,
I will fear no evil;

For You are with me;
Your rod and Your staff,
they comfort me."

Is it possible that in these same terms the members of a wolf pack, elk herd, or chimp troop also have a God (dominant male) to whom they pray (show submission) for the same purpose?

Epilogue

O, I got a zoo, I got a menagerie, inside my ribs, under my bony head, under my red-valve heart—and I got something else: it is a man-child heart, a woman-child heart: it is a father and mother and lover: it came from God-Knows-Where: it is going God-Knows-Where—For I am the keeper of the zoo: I say yes and no: I sing and kill and work: I am a pal of the world: I came from the wilderness.

Wilderness by Carl Sandburg

BIBLIOGRAPHY AND PERMISSIONS

The following books are the sources for quotes used in the text and are an excellent starting point for those interested in learning more about animal and human behavior and the people who study it. I am grateful to the publishers for allowing me to use copyrighted material.

Almost Human by Shirley Strum, Copyright © 1987 Shirley Strum, All Rights Reserved, Random House.

Animal Kitabu by Jean-Pierre Hallet, Copyright © 1967 Jean-Pierre Hallet, All Rights Reserved, Random House.

Carl Akeley, Africa's Collector, Africa's Savior, by Penelope Bodry-Sanders, Copyright © 1991 Penelope Bodry-Sanders, All Rights Reserved, Paragon House.

The Chimpanzees of Gombe by Jane Goodall, Copyright 1986 © the President and Fellows of Harvard College, Harvard University Press, All Rights Reserved.

The Chimps of Mt. Asserik, by Stella Brewer, Copyright © 1978 Stella Brewer, All Rights Reserved, Wm. Collins & Co. Ltd.

Dance of the Wolves by Roger Peters, Copyright © 1985 Roger Peters, All Rights Reserved, The McGraw-Hill Companies.

Elaine and Bill: Portrait of a Marriage, by Lee Hall, Copyright © 1993 Lee Hall, All Rights Reserved, HarperCollins Publishers.

Hearts of Darkness by Frank McLynn, Copyright © 1992 Frank McLynn, All Rights Reserved, Carroll and Graf Publishers, Inc.

Hit and Run by Nancy Griffin and Kim Masters, Copyright © 1996 Griffin and Masters, All Rights Reserved, Simon and Schuster.

The Hot House by Pete Earley, Copyright © 1992 Pete Earley, All Rights Reserved, Bantam Books.

In Praise of Wolves by R.D. Lawrence, Copyright © 1986 R.D. Lawrence, All Rights Reserved, Henry Holt and Company Inc. and Wallace Literary Agency.

In the Shadow of Man by Jane van Lawick-Goodall, Copyright © 1971 by Hugo and Jane van Lawick-Goodall, All Rights Reserved, Houghton Mifflin Company and Weidenfeld & Nicolson Ltd.

They Love and Kill Each Other by Vitus B. Droscher, translated by Jan Van Heurck Copyright © 1974 Hoffman und Campe Verlag, English translation Copyright © 1976 E.P. Dutton & Co., Inc. and W. H. Allen & Co. Ltd. Used by permission of Penguin Books USA Inc.

Never Cry Wolf by Farley Mowat, Copyright © 1963 Farley Mowat, Limited, All Rights Reserved, Little Brown and Company.

Through a Window by Jane Goodall. Copyright © Soko Publications ltd. All rights reserved Houghton Mifflin Company and Weidenfeld & Nicolson Ltd.

Up Among the Mountain Gorillas by Walter Baumgartel, Copyright © Walter Baumgartel, All Rights Reserved, Hawthorn Books/Red Dragon Press.

The Year of the Gorilla by George Schaller, Copyright © 1964 University of Chicago Press, All Rights Reserved.

INDEX